D0944547

THE PICTO

(pages 1 - 1(0)

SYMBOLS AND ABBREVIATIONS
USED IN THE MAPS

Route on motor road ⎯⎯⎯⎯⎯⎯⎯⎯⎯

Good footpath - - - - - - - - - - -
(sufficiently distinct to be followed in mist)

Intermittent footpath -.--.--.--.
(difficult to follow in mist)

No path; route recommended ·················

Wall ∞∞∞∞∞∞∞∞   **Broken Wall** o o o o o o o o o o

Fence +++++++++++   **Broken Fence** ''''''''''''''''''

Marshy ground   ⋅⋅⋅⋅⋅   **Trees** ♤♧♤♧♤♧

Crags ⋙⋙⋙   **Scree** ░░░   **Boulders** ⬡⬡⬡⬡

Stream or River ⌇⌇⌇⌇⌇⌇→
(arrow indicates direction of flow)

Waterfall ⌒⌒⌒⌒   **Bridge** ⌢⫞⫞

Buildings ▦   **Unenclosed road** ···········

Summit·cairn ▲   **Other** (prominent) **cairns**   △ △

Contours (at 100' intervals)   1600   1500

Map scale : 2½" = 1 mile
North is top of the page

Map continuation
(page number)   163

Abbreviations :   *PW* Pennine Way
OS Ordnance Survey   *O.C* Open Country
MCWW Manchester Corporation Water Works
PPPB Peak Park Planning Board

**Miles
from
Edale**   ⑫
(on main route only)

THE PICTORIAL GUIDES
TO THE
LAKELAND FELLS

PENNINE WAY
COMPANION

Malham Cove

PENNINE WAY COMPANION

A PICTORIAL GUIDE

aWainwright

PUBLISHED
by
FRANCES LINCOLN
LONDON

Frances Lincoln Limited
4 Torriano Mews
Torriano Avenue
London NW5 2RZ
www.franceslincoln.com

First published by Frances Lincoln
2004
Originally published by the Westmorland Gazette, 1968
Revised 1994

Printed in Thailand

ISBN 978 0 7112 2235 9

ACKNOWLEDGMENTS

The preliminary field-work for this book was undertaken in 1965 by four men, all experienced fellwalkers, who were each allotted a section of the Pennine Way to follow and explore, checking the official route with the information provided on the Ordnance maps and in publications of the National Parks Commission, the Ramblers' Association, the Youth Hostels Association, and of other authoritative sources, resolving existing doubts, and compiling detailed notes for my use subsequently in 1966 and 1967.

This work they did right well, and it is a pleasure to record their names and to pay a grateful tribute to them for all the assistance they gave.

The four men are

● HARRY APPLEYARD, of Wigton
   Born 1918. Chartered surveyor.
   Member of the Ramblers' Association.
   Section: Tan Hill to Cross Fell

● LEN CHADWICK, of Dobcross, near Oldham
   Born 1915. Shorthand-typist.
   Hon Secretary, Kindred Spirits Fellwalking Society
   Section: Edale to the Calder Valley

● CYRIL MOORE, of Morecambe
   Born 1912. Draughtsman and surveyor.
   Section: Cross Fell to Kirk Yetholm
      also Malham Tarn to Tan Hill

● LAWRENCE W. SMITH, of Deepcar, nr. Sheffield
   Born 1924. Office manager
   Section: The Calder Valley to Malham Tarn

Four good men and true!

....

Other friends assisted by conveying me in their cars to parts of the Pennine Way not served by public transport and accompanying me on my walks to see that my ageing feet did not stumble and that my wants were met: their solicitude was touching, their kindness unbounded.

These too have my grateful thanks.

This book is a team effort.   aw

PUBLISHER'S NOTE TO THE 2004 EDITION

The Pennine Way – England's first continuous long-distance path for walkers – runs for 268 miles along the length of the Pennines. Inaugurated in 1965, it has become one of the most popular long-distance footpaths in Britain, used by well over a hundred thousand walkers a year. *Pennine Way Companion* was first published in 1968. Over the years since then, heavy use has led to many parts of the route becoming seriously eroded and diversions have been set up to avoid the worst affected stretches. Walkers attempting the Pennine Way need to be aware of these changes. They need also to be aware that *Pennine Way Companion* advocates some shortcuts and diversions that are not part of the officially approved route. In some cases, the routes Wainwright suggested do not lie on rights of way.

In 2003, Frances Lincoln took on publication of the Wainwright guides and, with the approval of the Wainwright Estate, put in hand a major programme of updating. The programme will begin with Book One of the Pictorial Guides to the Lakeland Fells and further revised guides, with maps and text amended where needed by Chris Jesty, will be published over the coming years. However, a fully revised and updated edition of *Pennine Way Companion* will not be available until this programme is complete. In the meantime, believing that Wainwright's guide is better out of date than out of print, we are reissuing the existing edition. This was last updated by Chris Jesty in 1994. Detours and changes to the terrain that have taken place since 1994 are not indicated.

In this edition of *Pennine Way Companion*, Wainwright text that covers parts of the route that were invalid in 1994 is marked with a bold line in the left- or right-hand margins. An asterisk then leads to typeset copy describing the revised route, which appears, in the main, at the foot of the affected pages. On occasion the map has been slightly amended and no revised text appears. Walkers should always refer to the new text whenever they reach original copy marked with a bold line.

This guide has only been updated to 1994. Before planning to walk any section of the Pennine Way, walkers are strongly advised to consult up-to-date Ordnance Survey maps and to visit the Countryside Agency website – www.nationaltrail.co.uk/pennineway – for general safety advice and the latest information relevant to their intended route.

CONTENTS

What are these,
So wither'd, and so wild in their attire,
That look not like inhabitants o' the earth,
And yet are on't ?

SHAKESPEARE (Macbeth, Act I)

Crag Lough,
looking to
Hotbank Crags

INTRODUCTION

The Pennine Way was the happy inspiration, over thirty years ago, of Mr. Tom Stephenson, the present Secretary of the Ramblers' Association; but he did more than think of the idea: he worked hard to bring it into being. Many were the difficulties, and many were the objections, but all were overcome in a long and tedious campaign before Parliament set the seal of authority on a recommendation by the National Parks Commission and gave approval to this first long-distance right of way for walkers. Officially, Whitehall created the Pennine Way. But those who walk it should remember that it was one man who inspired, in his mind and by his patience and effort, the freedom they enjoy. Mr. Stephenson has served the cause of walkers well throughout a long life, but his name will most be revered for his imaginative conception of a continuous way for travellers on foot across half of England.

The terminal points of the Pennine Way are Edale, in Derbyshire, and Kirk Yetholm, just over the Scottish Border in Roxburghshire. The route enters or passes through all the northern counties of England: half the distance lies within the boundaries of Yorkshire, almost a third is in Northumberland, and the others are visited only briefly. Three National Parks (the Peak District, the Yorkshire Dales, and Northumberland) and a Nature Reserve (Moor House) are linked by the route.

The name "Pennine Way" is a fine, challenging one, an inspiration in itself and a clarion call, but it is not truly descriptive of the territory covered: the route is in fact a Pennine Way and a Cheviot Way combined — but only *partly* a Pennine Way and only *partly* a Cheviot Way. The Pennine Range is the backbone of northern England: it is a barrier of high ground between the coastal plains of the Irish Sea and the North Sea, an uplift of wild moorlands, mainly uninhabited, separating the industrial, densely populated areas to east and west. This high tract of land is terminated in the north by the Tyne Gap, and in the south by the flat country of the Midlands. A *true* Pennine Way would lie along the full length of the Pennine Range and would have better suited the name had it been confined between these extremities, taking in the lovely Derbyshire Dales and ending with the minor foothills east of Carlisle. This, apart from remedying the present inappropriateness of the name, would have improved the scenic qualities of the route. Neither Kirk Yetholm nor Edale have any features that make them obvious choices as termini : both are small villages without any outstanding characteristics or geographical highlights or historical importance. Better that the Pennine Way had been given the glorious entry to the hills provided by charming Dovedale as its starting point, and, as its thrilling finale, the exciting arrival at the Roman Wall! Then it would really have been a Pennine Way, the whole Pennine Way and nothing but the Pennine Way; and (minus the Cheviots) a more compact and rewarding expedition.

But this is merely a personal opinion (and the opinion of a chronic purist to boot!). There is no intention here to criticise or detract from the merits of the approved route — the *official* Pennine Way is a jolly good walk, no doubt at all about that.

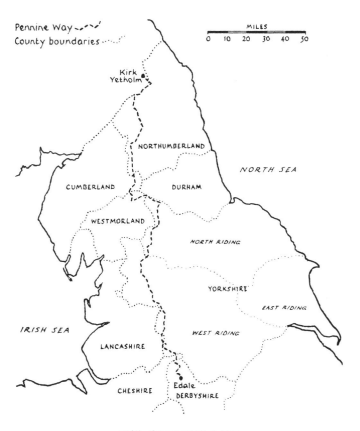

Pennine Way ·-·⌐·⌐·
County boundaries ·····

MILES
0 10 20 30 40 50

Kirk Yetholm

NORTHUMBERLAND

NORTH SEA

CUMBERLAND

DURHAM

WESTMORLAND

NORTH RIDING

YORKSHIRE

EAST RIDING

IRISH SEA

LANCASHIRE

WEST RIDING

CHESHIRE

Edale
DERBYSHIRE

THE PENNINE WAY
IN RELATION TO
THE COUNTIES OF NORTHERN ENGLAND

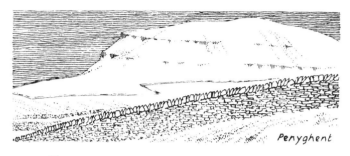

Penyghent

   The main watershed of northern England is the line
that divides the west-flowing streams (Irish Sea) and the
east-flowing streams (North Sea).   This watershed is,
naturally, the crest of the Pennine Range.   It is not an
arbitrary or imaginary line : obviously it exists although
not marked on maps and not often clearly defined on the
ground. It *must* exist, just as the law of gravity exists —
rain falling on the Pennines *must* run off by pre-destined
courses, *downhill,* and whether ultimately to east or west
depends on where it falls.   The *ideal* Pennine Way would
follow such a line, keeping always to the highest land ahead
and having west-flowing streams consistently on one hand
and east-flowing streams on the other ; and, because of
the complicated topography of the hills, its course would
by no means always be on a north-south axis.   The
Pennines are predominantly flat-topped, not sharply ridged,
and the watershed is in places simply a morass of stagnant
pools, but at some point there is movement, east or west,
and the line of demarcation would need to be determined.
   A walk of this nature, keeping strictly to the main
watershed, would be extremely arduous, for it is along the
tops of these moors, especially those with a peat covering,
that progress is most difficult.   Constant reference to
maps would be necessary ; there are few paths ;   lodgings
and places of refreshment are non-existent. This would be
an undertaking only for the toughest and most resolute of
he-men carrying food and shelter on their backs.
   The route of the Pennine Way is kinder.   Only rarely
does it coincide with the main watershed and then never
for long before deflecting to the easier flanks, generally
the less steep and gentler eastern slopes.

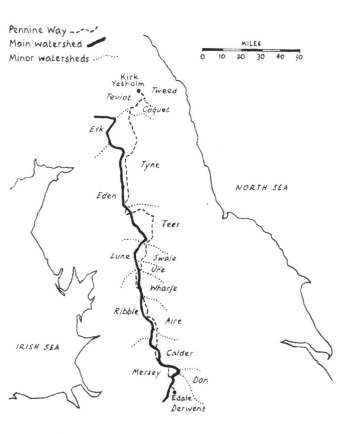

Pennine Way - - - -
Main watershed
Minor watersheds ....

MILES
0 10 20 30 40 50

Kirk Yetholm
Tweed
Teviot
Coquet
Esk
Tyne
NORTH SEA
Eden
Tees
Lune
Swale
Ure
Wharfe
Ribble
Aire
IRISH SEA
Calder
Mersey
Don
Edale
Derwent

THE PENNINE WAY
IN RELATION TO
THE MAIN WATERSHED OF NORTHERN ENGLAND

East Gill Force, Keld

The Pennine Way is both a high-level route and a wilderness walk, but not exclusively so. There are lengthy sections where the Way crosses or accompanies cultivated valleys and lowlands, notably in the Aire Gap and Northumberland, and other sections that would be more properly described as riverside rambles: the River Tees and the River South Tyne in particular are closely followed for several miles in flowery meadows. But in general the route seeks out the lonely moors, preferring the solitude of the heights. Even so, the route can reach no greater elevation than the hills themselves — and the Pennines are squat and sprawling rather than lofty. The diagrams opposite show that while four-fifths of the Way is at a height greater than 1000', only one-quarter of it is above 1500' and only in eight places is 2000' exceeded. It is not *altitude* but the *nature of the terrain* that creates difficulties of progress, especially on the peat moors of the Peak and west Yorkshire, where the walking, in mires and heather at around 1500' is much more arduous than, for instance, on the firmer footing of Cross Fell, which at 2930' is the highest point reached by the route. The Pennine Way is rough walking, but not mountaineering.

vii

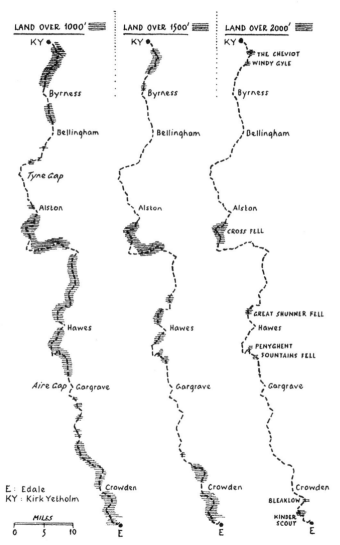

* Map revised 1994 to show new route at Edale.

The Pennine Way pursues an erratic course: erratic in the sense that the route does not adhere to an inflexible compass bearing between its terminal points but deviates so considerably that, at some stage or other, every direction on the compass is in one's sights: north, south, east and west and all intermediate bearings. Walking it is like playing a gigantic game of snakes and ladders. As an example: after the long crossing from Teesdale to Dufton, a hard day's walk in itself, the ultimate objective is further away at supper than it was at breakfast. It is 150 miles from Edale to Kirk Yetholm, measuring a *straight* line on the map, yet to get to one place from the other on the Pennine Way almost twice that distance must be walked.

Limestone pavement above Malham Cove

Officially the length of the Pennine Way is 250 miles, a nice round figure, but obviously too nice and too round to be accurate. It is *approximately* correct, *measuring the route on a map*, but does not *sufficiently* take account of ups and downs and ins and outs. The rises and falls on the route are persistent yet not steep enough to influence the mileage more than slightly, but the curves and zigzags of such paths as do exist and the trials and errors where they don't, the endless deviations around rough or boggy ground and searchings for escape from awkward places, the inevitable mists : all these add to the distance afoot and are not provided for in a count based on map-miles. Of course, the Pennine Way can never be measured with absolute accuracy. In the maps in this Guide, an attempt has been made to indicate the miles *of walking*, one by one, taking into account the contours and the nature of the ground, and the total is 270, not 250...... ✱ Taking further into account the recommended detours to places of special interest near the route, and the extra miles walked off-route in search of beds and breakfasts (and less worthy attractions such as beer and sex) it is likely that the mileage per individual will be around 300.

Inevitably, but mistakenly, the Pennine Way will be subject to record-breaking. Somebody, someday, will write to the papers to proclaim that he has walked the distance in 10 days. Then somebody else will better that, and so on. In due course the record will be reckoned in split seconds. All this is *wrong*. The Pennine Way was never intended to be a race against time. No, to be enjoyed (and why else do it?) it should be done leisurely. There is much to observe, much to explore, much to learn. The Way leads its followers to places of historical interest, of spectacular landscapes, of great charm and beauty; and even on the bare hilltops there is the study of the topography and the distant views to engage the attention. There are rich fields of exploration for the botanist and geologist and antiquarian, while for the ordinary mortal careful observation of the countryside, the wide panoramas, the flowers and the wild life, means an enrichment of knowledge and greater understanding.

If the Pennine Way passed through unchanging scenery it would be a treadmill. But its main appeal is *variety*. You pass, day after day, into fresh scenes, new worlds of enquiry. They should not be entered or left in a hurry.....

You may not come this way again.

*The length of the walk has changed a little due to the revised routes at the start and at Wessenden.

There are two methods of tackling the Pennine Way.

The most usual is to do it at "one fell swoop" as a single walk. This entails the greater hardship and privation but is the more challenging, the more adventurous, the more satisfying upon completion, besides providing a thrilling story that can be told over and over again in later years to long-suffering grandchildren.

There is nothing in the rules to say that the Pennine Way must be done at one go, though this is generally understood. The other method is to do it in bits, a section at a time, not necessarily in sequence. Such an arrangement makes the walk possible for those who cannot conveniently find the three consecutive weeks necessary to do the journey in one expedition, and, apart from this, has certain other things in its favour: (a) advantage can be taken of fine weather, (b) only a light load, if any at all, need be carried, (c) excuses are provided for getting away from the wife* on some 30 to 40 occasions, (d) the pleasure of achievement is extended over a longer period, even a year or two, (e) it becomes possible for persons who can walk only a few miles at a time to complete the full journey, (f) sections may be done in any order and in either direction as and when most convenient. For those with cars this method is especially suitable: as the diagram opposite shows, the Pennine Way is crossed by motor roads throughout its length, usually at quiet places where there can be no objection to parking a car while a section is walked. [To avoid retracing steps, an ideal arrangement would be for two car-owners to work as a team, so that each can walk across country to the other's car (passing him en route) and return in it to a rendezvous fixed in advance]. Using this method, many can walk the Pennine Way who may have thought they would never get an opportunity of doing so. A suggested 'break-down' of the Way into sections bounded by motor roads is given in the "Reader's Log" at the end of the book.

* Sorry, girls! I shouldn't have said that, should I?

The cliffs of High Cup

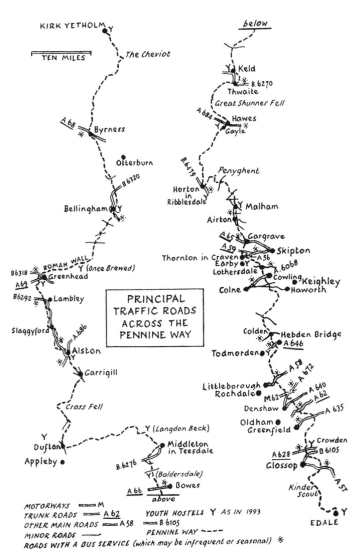

Navigation, the following of the desired route *exactly*, is the major problem. The Pennine Way is not a continuous footpath : more often there is no path at all. The special finger-posts are insufficient and irregular: a section of nine miles without one (Great Shunner Fell) is succeeded by ten within the next mile (Thwaite). Cairns on the high ground are infrequent. Ordnance maps make only a half-hearted attempt to show the route approximately. Oddly, the most perplexing sections are in the valleys, amongst the fields and habitations, where a wrong stile can lead one badly astray to incur the wrath of the farmer — and not all the farmers, understandably, are in sympathy with the Pennine Way. And it is apparent from accounts of the journey already published that the writers have not consistently walked in each other's footsteps.

It was soon clear to the author, after initial forays, that his Guide should concentrate on making manifestly obvious the correct thread in the web of complications — and this could only be done by providing a continuous map on a scale large enough to indicate *in detail* (showing walls, fences, stiles, gates, etc.) these more confusing passages, a running commentary being included for good measure. To do this, the features of the countryside *off-route*, desirable but not really necessary, had to be sacrificed. The result is a map in the form of a strip that should enable anyone to walk the Pennine Way without putting a foot wrong, but tell him next to nothing of the country alongside or around. Like walking in blinkers! It is recommended, therefore, that this deficiency be remedied by the use, in conjunction with the Guide, of the relevant 1" Ordnance Survey maps (as listed below). to appreciate more fully the geography of the immediate district and identify distant features in view on the route. The Guide will tell you which field you are in, the Ordnance map which valley. The Guide will identify the stile ahead, but if you want to know where the hell you really are in relation to the nearest public house it's the map you need.

O.S. LANDRANGER MAPS COVERING THE PENNINE WAY

SHEET 74 (Kelso)	SHEET 98 (Wensleydale)
" 80 (Cheviot Hills)	" 103 (Blackburn and Burnley)
86 (Haltwhistle)	" 109 (Manchester)
91 (Appleby)	" 110 (Sheffield and
92 (Barnard Castle)	Huddersfield)

Early summer is the best time of the year for walking the Pennine Way in its entirety: then, there is a better chance of settled weather, the hours of daylight are long and there is no prohibition of access to the grouse-shooting moors crossed by the route in its southern reaches. Not to be considered is a *winter* journey (except for short sections in good weather): the days are too brief, conditions can be Arctic in severity on the higher ground, deep snow could bring progress to a standstill. Nor is it, at any time, really an undertaking for a solitary walker: a companion of like interests and ability is preferable, one who can be endured without strain on the nerves, who can smile in adversity.

The Pennine Way offers you the experience of a lifetime, which is *not* to say that it offers you continuous enjoyment. It is a tough, bruising walk and the compensations are few. You do it because you want to prove to yourself that you are man enough to do it. You do it to get it off your conscience. You do it because you count it a personal achievement. Which it is, precisely.

Gritstone rocks
on Goldsborough

The Border Hotel, Kirk Yetholm

The Terminal Hotels

The Old Nag's Head, Edale

THE PICTORIAL GUIDE
(pages 1 - 176)

SYMBOLS AND ABBREVIATIONS
USED IN THE MAPS

Route on motor road

Good footpath
(sufficiently distinct to be followed in mist)

Intermittent footpath
(difficult to follow in mist)

No path; route recommended

Wall   Broken Wall

Fence   Broken Fence

Marshy ground   Trees

Crags   Scree   Boulders

Stream or River
(arrow indicates direction of flow)

Waterfall   Bridge

Buildings   Unenclosed road

Summit·cairn ▲   Other (prominent) cairns   △ △

Contours (at 100' intervals)   ·····1600·····
·····1500·····

Map scale: 2½"= 1 mile   Map continuation
North is top of the page   (page number) 163

Abbreviations: P.W.: Pennine Way
OS: Ordnance Survey   O.C: Open Country   Miles
MCWW: Manchester Corporation Water Works   from   ⑫
PPPB: Peak Park Planning Board   Edale
(on main route only)

THE PLAN OF THE GUIDE
THESE NOTES ARE IMPORTANT

The design of this Guide is unusual (by Western standards of book-making) and must be understood before reference is made to the following pages. A Guide is supposed to help, not confuse. This one will help if it is used as it is intended to be used.

The Pennine Way follows a course lying between two terminal points, one (Edale) south of the other (Kirk Yetholm) and either may be regarded as the start of the Way and the other the end. However, all authorities refer to Edale as the starting-point, i.e. they assume that the walk will be done from south to north. There is no logical reason for this, but in fact it is preferable to start at Edale, walking north away from the prevailing weather: it is always easier to walk with the rain and wind and sun coming from behind. *This Guide is based on the assumption that the walker using it will start at Edale and finish at Kirk Yetholm, and the notes accompanying the maps are written accordingly.*

Now about the maps. Actually there is one only, continuous throughout the Guide, but because it is on a generous scale (2½ inches to a mile) it occupies no fewer than 84 pages (pages 5 to 171, *odd numbers only*). It is presented in the form of a strip, with all the information necessary to follow the Way exactly. But geographical details *off-route* are omitted; this is why the 1" Ordnance maps should be used in addition, to give a fuller appraisal of the countryside in sight beyond the environs of the route and to establish the position of the walker in relation to the district he is passing through.

In all published maps, *north is traditionally at the top*, the left side is *west*, the right side *east*, and *south* is at the bottom. We are so used to this arrangement that any other is unthinkable. We are also taught to read from left to right, and from top to bottom, i.e. *downwards*.

You DON'T have to stand on your head to use this Guide

Anyone travelling *south to north* (against the grain, so to speak) will therefore read *upwards* on the map he is using; and in this Guide, too, a walker starting at Edale will need to follow each map-section up the page. When he walks off the top of the page, where does the map continue? Well, in this Guide (and this is the funny thing about it) the map continues on the next *odd-number* page *preceding*—at the bottom, of course. Thus, starting at Edale, which is found at the foot of page 171, the map proceeds up-page and is continued on page 169, where it goes up-page and continues on page 167, and so on. Ultimately, if you don't give up or get lost, you will arrive at Kirk Yetholm at the top of page 5.

Is this a logical arrangement? On the face of it, NO: it means that the end of the map occurs at the start of the Guide, on page 5, and the beginning is on the last page, 171. Actually, YES: the walk is being done *contra* and the map must follow suit. It seems to make sense, that if a map is read upwards its continuation should precede, not follow. This argument is supported by the result: a perfectly orderly progression from *north to south*, *with* the grain, in *natural* sequence. If the start was made at Kirk Yetholm, then the map would read *downwards* from the top of page 5 and onwards to the end at Edale on page 171, just like reading a book. It is only because the walk is being done in reverse, *i.e. south to north*, that the map-pages are arranged back to front. [There is no valid reason, of course, why the walk should not be done from north to south, and some people prefer to do so, but this Guide is designed for the majority, and the majority start from Edale. A north-to-south walker will be able to use the map with equal facility, and the illustrations will fall naturally into place, but the notes, insofar as they amplify the route, will be a source of annoyance, directions needing to be reversed].

Is this clear? Well, never mind: it will become clear as you go along.

.... *and you DON'T have to walk backwards.*

Just one other thing: *Page 4 is intended exclusively for heroes, and you are put on your honour NOT to read it unless and until you duly reach Kirk Yetholm.*

4

The End

When you reach the village green in Kirk Yetholm, you can halt your legs, enjoy a rest on the public seat under the trees, and look back along the road that brought you here.....and reflect awhile.

Youth Hostel, Kirk Yetholm

You have completed a mission and achieved an ambition. You have walked the Pennine Way, as you dreamed of doing. This will be a very satisfying moment in your life. You will be tired and hungry and travel-stained. But you will feel great, just great.

There is no brass band to greet you; there is nobody waiting to pin a medal on your breast. There may be people about but they will take no notice of you. Nobody cares that you have walked, and just this minute completed, the Pennine Way. You will not get your name in the papers, nor be interviewed for television. No, the satisfaction you feel is intensely personal, and cannot be shared: the sense of achievement is yours alone simply because you have earned it alone. Others cannot understand. Indeed, it may well happen that, returned to 'civilisation' (so called), you will for a time feel lonelier than ever you did in the wilderness of mountain and moorland. But you will go on feeling great.

It will be the same when you get back home. When you tell your friends that you have walked the Pennine Way they will not jump for joy: more likely they will look at you out of the corner of their eyes and whisper amongst themselves. Many will want to ask "What *is* the Pennine Way?" but will say instead, to spare your feelings, "Oh, really?" Your mother will be proud of you, as she will of all your accomplishments, but for all the acclaim you get from others you might as well keep the news a secret.

Well, anyway, you didn't walk the Pennine Way to please other people. You did it because it was a challenge and you wanted to see whether you could do it. You wanted to test yourself. You didn't do it to earn memories, but memories you will have, and in abundance, for the rest of your life, highlighting past days. You will find you have enriched yourself. You will be more ready to tackle other big ventures and more able to bring them to a successful conclusion. You have learned not to give up.

You will be a better man *because you have walked the Pennine Way.*

Well done!
AW

THE END
OF THE
ROAD

*Bus for Kelso
waiting*

(a) *WHITE LAW TO KIRK YETHOLM*
(b) *HALTERBURNHEAD TO KIRK YETHOLM*   Landranger **Sheet 74**

Kirk Yetholm would seem a lovely village to anyone who had walked 270 miles to reach it even if it were slums and slagheaps. But in fact it *is* a lovely village: its setting in a pleasant valley is enhanced by trim cottages around a green, an attractive inn, an old pinnacled church and a quiet but friendly atmosphere. In former times it was a meeting place and camping ground for an ancient clan of gipsies, and traces of their occupation remain.

Today it is a peaceful sanctuary, its main link with the busier world beyond being the bus service to Kelso.

Kirk Yetholm
Youth Hostel
Border Hotel
WOOLER
(270)
Kirk
Shop
to KELSO
← STOP! This is the end. Son, you have walked the Pennine Way.
100 yards to go
30 m.p.h. sign SLOW DOWN!
chalet
First view of Kirk Yetholm. At last!
400 yards to go
raspberries on the roadside
The road climbs 150 feet from the cattle grid — the cruellest hill of all. Get up off your knees. Don't give in. The agony will soon be over.
Take a last long look back
1200 yards to go
1300 yards to go
1400 yards to go
1500 yards to go
(269)
barn
cattle grid
HIGH LEVEL ROUTE
hill fort
ROAD
Halter Burn
barn
bracken
across
HIGH LEVEL ROUTE
hill fort comes into view →
(268)
signpost gate
BORDER FENCE
Peniel Centre
The banks of the stream are fringed with musk, a plant more associated with domestic gardens.
As the path descends from the border fence, the concentric ramparts of the Iron Age hill fort on Green Humbleton can be seen directly ahead.
Whitelaw Nick
signpost
White Law
LOW LEVEL ROUTE ROAD
cattle grid
barn
shed
across
7
Halterburnhead (farm)
7

Positively the last lap. Honestly.

Looking back to The Cheviot (left) and The Schil

Every walker likes to measure his progress by looking back over the way he has come, and there is special satisfaction in doing so on the Pennine Way, where every mile counts. The viewpoint for the above drawing is the col between The Curr and Black Hag: here is the last view of the Cheviot hills before the route drops to the valleys and they are lost to sight.

The summit of The Schil

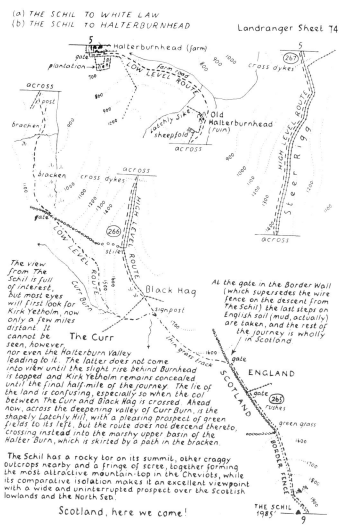

(a) THE SCHIL TO WHITE LAW
(b) THE SCHIL TO HALTERBURNHEAD

Landranger Sheet 74

The view from The Schil is full of interest, but most eyes will first look for Kirk Yetholm, now only a few miles distant. It cannot be seen, however, nor even the Halterburn Valley leading to it. The latter does not come into view until the slight rise behind Burnhead is topped and Kirk Yetholm remains concealed until the final half-mile of the journey. The lie of the land is confusing, especially so when the col between The Curr and Black Hag is crossed. Ahead now, across the deepening valley of Curr Burn, is the shapely Latchly Hill, with a pleasing prospect of green fields to its left, but the route does not descend thereto, crossing instead into the marshy upper basin of the Halter Burn, which is skirted by a path in the bracken.

At the gate in the Border Wall (which supersedes the wire fence on the descent from The Schil) the last steps on English soil (mud, actually) are taken, and the rest of the journey is wholly in Scotland.

The Schil has a rocky tor on its summit, other craggy outcrops nearby and a fringe of scree, together forming the most attractive mountain-top in the Cheviots, while its comparative isolation makes it an excellent viewpoint with a wide and uninterrupted prospect over the Scottish lowlands and the North Sea.

Scotland, here we come!

The High Level Route is the main route and the finest way to finish the walk. The Low Level Route is recommended if time is pressing, as it is likely to be at this stage.

Page revised 1994.

8

Hen Hole

'Stone Men' near Auchope Cairn

Auchope Cairn

The Schil

CAIRN HILL (WEST TOP) TO THE SCHIL

The section from the acute angle in the fence on Cairn Hill west top to the interesting summit of Auchope Cairn is a morass of juicy peat, but thereafter the walking improves vastly on firm dry grass. It is good going all the way to The Schil, the rocky tor of which is clearly in view, but there is little of interest apart from the craggy fastnesses of Hen Hole, which can be viewed by a short detour from the fence halfway down the slope from Auchope Cairn: this scene is impressively wild. Note also from the head of Red Cribs an exquisite view northwards along the valley of College Burn.

All streams are now heading for the north, Tweedwards.

The detour to The Cheviot

The Cheviot is the highest but the least attractive of the Border hills, and it is unfortunate that the official route of the Pennine Way prescribes a detour to its summit, coming as it does at a critical stage of a very long trek. Most walkers will arrive at the west top of Cairn Hill, where the detour starts, already tired, and will, if favoured by survival and after due passage of valuable time, return to the said west top of Cairn Hill none the richer but a good deal wearier after floundering for two miles through filthy and pathless peathags that demolish the spirit and defeat the flesh without even the reward of a good view. Indeed they may even find, after the toils of getting there, that the Ordnance column on the summit, which stands on a grass mound in a sea of squelchy black ooze, is inaccessible because of bad conditions underfoot. 26 miles plus The Cheviot is too much for ordinary mortals. The Cheviot stands well away from the Border, wholly in England, and after experiencing it one can readily understand why the Scots wanted no part of it.

Do it for the record or to satisfy conscience, if you must, but do not expect to enjoy it. In mist or rain, give it a miss altogether.

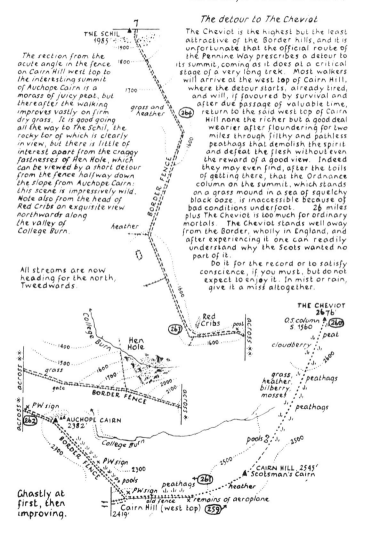

Ghastly at first, then improving.

A typical sign erected by the Ramblers' Association and supported by turves of peat, near King's Seat, looking to Score Head. Many such signs in the vicinity of Cairn Hill have been wantonly 'beheaded'.

The acute angle in the Border Fence on Cairn Hill west top, looking to The Cheviot.

Tumulus near the fence on Windy Gyle, north-east of Russell's Cairn

The Cheviot, from Russell's Cairn

WINDY GYLE TO CAIRN HILL (WEST TOP)

Landranger Sheet 80

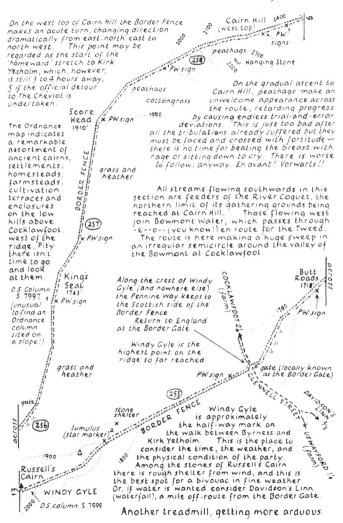

On the west top of Cairn Hill the Border Fence makes an acute turn, changing direction dramatically from east-north-east to north-west. This point may be regarded as the start of the 'homeward' stretch to Kirk Yetholm, which, however, is still 3 to 4 hours away, 5 if the official detour to The Cheviot is undertaken.

Cairn Hill (west top)
peathags
Hanging Stone
PW signs

The Ordnance map indicates a remarkable assortment of ancient cairns, settlements, homesteads, farmsteads, cultivation terraces and enclosures on the low hills above Cocklawfoot, west of the ridge. Pity there isn't time to go and look at them.

Score Head 1910'
PW sign
peathags
cottongrass

On the gradual ascent to Cairn Hill, peathags make an unwelcome appearance across the route, retarding progress by causing endless trial-and-error deviations. This is just too bad after all the tribulations already suffered but they must be faced and crossed with fortitude — there is no time for beating the breast with rage or sitting down to cry. There is worse to follow, anyway. En avant! Vorwärts!!

BORDER FENCE

grass and heather

All streams flowing southwards in this section are feeders of the River Coquet, the northern limit of its gathering grounds being reached at Cairn Hill. Those flowing west join Bowmont Water, which passes through -e--o-- (you know!) en route for the Tweed. The route is here making a huge sweep in an irregular semicircle around the valley of the Bowmont at Cocklawfoot.

PW sign

O.S. Column S.7997 (unusual to find an Ordnance column sited on a slope!)

King's Seat 1743'
PW sign

Along the crest of Windy Gyle (and nowhere else) the Pennine Way keeps to the Scottish side of the Border Fence
Return to England at the Border Gate

Windy Gyle is the highest point on the ridge so far reached.

Butt Roads 1718'
PW sign

grass and heather

gate (locally known as the Border Gate)
PW sign

CLENNELL STREET

DAVIDSON'S LINN

USWAYFORD (farm)

gate

across

stone shelter
tumulus (star marker)

BORDER FENCE

Windy Gyle is approximately the half-way mark on the walk between Byrness and Kirk Yetholm. This is the place to consider the time, the weather, and the physical condition of the party. Among the stones of Russell's Cairn there is rough shelter from wind, and this is the best spot for a bivouac in fine weather. Or, if water is wanted, consider Davidson's Linn (waterfall), a mile off-route from the Border Gate.

Russell's Cairn
WINDY GYLE
O.S. column S.7999

Another treadmill, getting more arduous.

above : *Russell's Cairn*

right : *The Rowhope Valley as seen from the ridge*

below :

The view ahead from Beefstand Hill

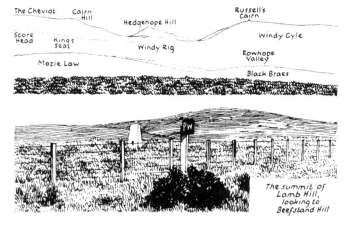

The Cheviot   Cairn Hill

Hedgehope Hill

Russell's Cairn

Score Head

King's Seat

Windy Rig

Windy Cyle

Rowhope Valley

Mozie Law

Black Braes

The summit of Lamb Hill, looking to Beefstand Hill

LAMB HILL TO WINDY GYLE

The undulations in this section are slight and the walking is easy apart from a few roughnesses and marshy patches, but the route lacks interest and is tedious and tiring. Ahead, Russell's Cairn is prominent but never seems to get any nearer. The views on all sides are excellent and far-ranging.

Russell's Cairn, one of the largest on British hills, is an antiquity (a tumulus). Set in the massive pile of stones is a star marker, a rough wind-shelter and an Ordnance column. Its altitude is variously given as 2034' and 2036'.

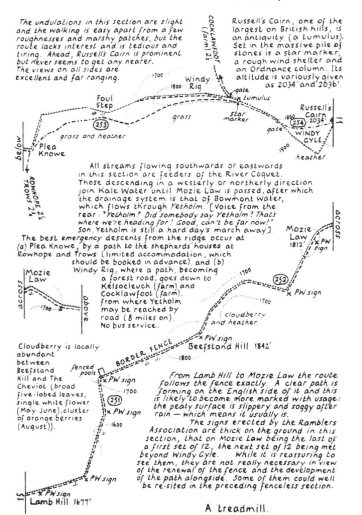

All streams flowing southwards or eastwards in this section are feeders of the River Coquet. Those descending in a westerly or northerly direction join Kale Water until Mozie Law is passed, after which the drainage system is that of Bowmont Water, which flows through Yetholm. [Voice from the rear: "Yetholm? Did somebody say Yetholm? That's where we're heading for! Good, can't be far now!" Son, Yetholm is still a hard day's march away]

The best emergency descents from the ridge occur at (a) Plea Knowe, by a path to the shepherds' houses at Rowhope and Trows (limited accommodation, which should be booked in advance) and (b) Windy Rig, where a path, becoming a forest road, goes down to Kelsocleuch (farm) and Cocklawfoot (farm), from where Yetholm may be reached by road (8 miles on). No bus service.

Cloudberry is locally abundant between Beefstand Hill and The Cheviot (broad five-lobed leaves, single white flower (May-June), cluster of orange berries (August)).

From Lamb Hill to Mozie Law the route follows the fence exactly. A clear path is forming on the English side of it and this is likely to become more marked with usage: the peaty surface is slippery and soggy after rain — which means it usually is.

The signs erected by the Ramblers Association are thick on the ground in this section, that on Mozie Law being the last of a first set of 12, the next set of 12 being met beyond Windy Gyle. While it is reassuring to see them, they are not really necessary in view of the renewal of the fence and the development of the path alongside. Some of them could well be re-sited in the preceding fenceless section.

A treadmill.

The walk along the Border

The final stage of the Pennine Way, from Byrness to Kirk Yetholm, is the longest and loneliest of all, and the Ordnance map should be studied very carefully before attempting it, noting contours and elevations, the main watersheds and destination of streams and inhabited valleys. No amount of pre-study, however, can anticipate the rigours of this walk.

From the Signal Station onwards the route lies almost entirely along a ridge forming the boundary between Scotland and England, over a succession of minor hills culminating in three main summits: Windy Gyle, The Cheviot and The Schil, each of which is surrounded and very substantially buttressed by outliers extending over a wide area, the whole mass being scored by deep valleys and innumerable watercourses. This tract of high land is remarkably extensive, and, on a first visit, confusing, with many lateral ridges branching off the principal watershed and often rising to a greater height, so that in places it is difficult to determine the position of the main ridge, which, to add to the doubt, not only switchbacks up and down but zigzags in and out of its general axis very considerably.

Fortunately for the walker's peace of mind the main ridge is accompanied throughout by a wire fence, recently renewed, and if this be kept close at hand there is no cause for straying, even in bad weather. This fence, quite an ordinary one, is known as the Border Fence, but it does not everywhere exactly mark the boundary, which it crosses several times within narrow limits of deviation. Nor does the route of the Pennine Way everywhere exactly coincide with either the fence or the boundary, some angles and corners being short-cut either officially or through usage, while on The Cheviot itself the route breaks clear away from both to pay honour to this highest summit in the group.

The full walk of 29 miles is too long for any but strong and tireless walkers to perform in one day: this is rough country and two miles an hour is a good pace on the worst sections of it. If the weather is calm a bivouac should be sought in the neighbourhood of Windy Gyle (halfway) and this is also the best camp-site if a tent is being carried. Nowhere on or near the main ridge is there an habitation or other form of building to provide shelter; nor are there any rocks to crawl under or holes to creep into. The other alternatives are to keep plodding on, thinking of Scott's journey to the South Pole, until overcome by exhaustion, and then lie down to die; or to descend into one or other of the many side-valleys in search of a bed: if the latter course is contemplated, it must be realised that a long descent is involved before the first habitation (usually a sheep farm) is reached, whichever valley is selected, that few of these provide accommodation — and, most important, that the whole deviation must be retraced next morning, adding many miles to the journey; or to arrange for a car to be waiting at some convenient road-end rendezvous. The points at which the ridge may best be left are indicated on the maps.

Make no mistake about it.

This is a long, hard walk. Damned long. Damned hard. Especially in rain.

KIRK YETHOLM

— The Border

– – The Pennine Way where it deviates from the Border

MILES

1985 THE SCHIL

THE CHEVIOT 2676

2382

1910

1743
1718

1842 2034
1812

WINDY GYLE

1842

1677
1590
1572

1512 ROMAN SIGNAL STATION

CHEW GREEN

CHEW GREEN TO LAMB HILL

Landranger Sheet 80

Streams flowing eastwards in this section of the route join the River Coquet down gentle slopes and reach the tarred road running along its valley to Alwinton — half a day's journey on foot.

West of the Border Fence, streams flow more steeply to the valley of Kale Water, which has a tarred road to Hownam and Morebattle — half a day's journey on foot.

The best emergency descent from the ridge in the vicinity of Chew Green is by the new road east of the Roman Camps, to Coquetdale; or, in the vicinity of Black Halls, by continuing along Dere Street to the valley of Kale Water at Tow Ford.

The two miles from the gate on Dere Street to the point where the fence is rejoined beyond Rennies Burn are difficult to follow with certainty even in clear weather, the PW signs being too widely spaced. The fence here makes a long detour to the west, but the Pennine Way cuts across to Lamb Hill more directly.

below

1300

More cairns are needed along here. In mist it would be safer to keep to the fence.

1400

grass and heather.

no track

PW sign

beware ditches.

thin track in rough grass and heather

(248)

TOW FORD (via Dere Street) (grass track) Tarred road at Tow Ford, goes north to Hownam 4 miles further. No bus service.

gate in angle of fence. Do NOT use it. Leave Dere Street at this point and aim for the next PW sign seen ahead.

Black Halls

The Border is reached again at the Roman Signal Station gate in fence gives access to it. Here is the first view of the valleys and hills west of the watershed

O.S. column S 1989 R

Lamb Hill 1677

13

PW sign

A (below) to BUCHTRIG (farm)

BORDER FENCE

1600

1500

BORDER FENCE

across

PW sign

BORDER FENCE

(250)

BLINDBURN (farm)

gate

A

1400

1400

1500

across

ROMAN SIGNAL STATION

circular sheepfold

Rennies Burn

grass heather, bilberry and mosses

(249)

PW sign

1400

1600

1664

Brownhart Law

x PW sign (the first of a series of 24 erected by the Ramblers Association)

DERE STREET ROMAN ROAD

(247)

At Chew Green, 'star markers' indicate items of antiquarian interest. Others will be seen en route later.

grass and rushes

above

F W

PW sign erected by the Ramblers Association (Northern Area)

Star marker, Chew Green

1500

groove

1400

Chew Sike

Chew Green ROMAN CAMPS

17

Interesting at first, then uninspiring.

Map slightly amended 1994.

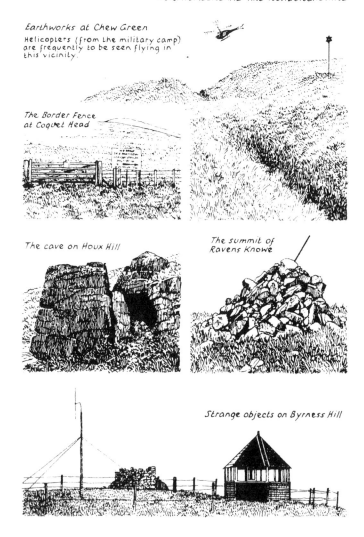

Earthworks at Chew Green

Helicopters (from the military camp) are frequently to be seen flying in this vicinity.

The Border Fence at Coquet Head

The cave on Houx Hill

The summit of Ravens Knowe

Strange objects on Byrness Hill

BYRNESS TO CHEW GREEN

Landranger Sheet 80

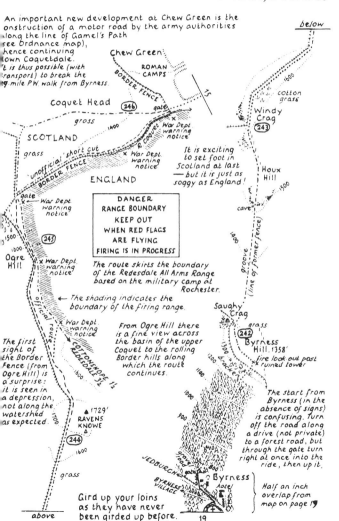

An important new development at Chew Green is the construction of a motor road by the army authorities along the line of Gamel's Path (see Ordnance map), hence continuing down Coquetdale. It is thus possible (with transport) to break the 29 mile PW. walk from Byrness.

Coquet Head (24b)

gross

SCOTLAND

grass

unofficial short cut

BORDER FENCE

ENGLAND

Chew Green

ROMAN CAMPS

BORDER FENCE

gate

× War Dept. warning notice

Coquet

× War Dept. warning notice

It is exciting to set foot in Scotland at last — but it is just as soggy as England!

gate War Dept. warning notice

(245)

Ogre Hill

× War Dept. warning notice

DANGER
RANGE BOUNDARY
KEEP OUT
WHEN RED FLAGS
ARE FLYING
FIRING IS IN PROGRESS

The route skirts the boundary of the Redesdale All Arms Range based on the military camp at Rochester.

← The shading indicates the boundary of the firing range.

War Dept. warning notice

The first sight of the Border Fence (from Ogre Hill) is a surprise: it is seen in a depression, not along the watershed as expected.

COTTONSHOPE   REDESDALE 12

▲ 1729' RAVENS KNOWE

(244)

grass

From Ogre Hill there is a fine view across the basin of the upper Coquet to the rolling Border hills along which the route continues.

below

1600

cotton grass

Windy Crag (243)

Houx Hill

1500

cave

groove (line of former fence)

Saughy Crag (242)

grass

Byrness Hill, 1358' fire look out past ruined tower

The start from Byrness (in the absence of signs) is confusing. Turn off the road along a drive (not private) to a forest road, but through the gate turn right at once into the ride, then up it.

JEDBURGH

BYRNESS VILLAGE

Byrness hotel

Half an inch overlap from map on page 19

Gird up your loins as they have never been girded up before.

19

Byrness Church

Footbridge and ford,
River Rede, Byrness

Blakehopeburnhaugh

BLAKEHOPEBURNHAUGH TO BYRNESS   Landranger Sheet 80

Byrness is an important stage of the Pennine Way, none more so. It is the last community before the final long walk of 29 miles over the wild and uninhabited Cheviot Hills to the finish at Kirk Yetholm. There is not much of it: a church, a good licensed hotel, a couple of private houses, a café in which Pennine wayfarers will be mightily interested alongside a filling station in which they will not, and, half a mile up the main road, and off-route, a new forestry village of 47 dwellings. The road is the fast and busy A 68 (Edinburgh-Newcastle): crossing it is the last traffic hazard; it would be damned annoying to get killed here with victory only a day's march away. The hamlet is almost choked by surrounding forests.

Accommodation is obtainable at the Byrness Hotel, which is open all the year round, and is advisedly booked in advance: a difficult thing to arrange when progress is dependent on the weather, but a telephone call from Bellingham before leaving there, may suffice.

The rucksack should be amply stocked with emergency rations before departing from Byrness, because the walk to Kirk Yetholm from this point is not only the longest stretch of the Pennine Way without a habitation, but one of the toughest, a test of endurance.

The casualty rate is high

The shy and graceful creatures with white tails, often to be seen in the river meadows hereabouts, are not big rabbits.

They are roe deer.

Cottonshopeburn Foot to Byrness:

The most frustrating mile of all! The official route crosses Cottonshope Burn near the farm and proceeds along the north-east bank of the Rede to Byrness. This section, however, has not been prepared for pedestrian travel (up to mid-1967). A footbridge and six stiles are needed before the walk becomes practicable. Barbed wire, impenetrable trees, shoulder-high vegetation and an angry farmer make it a desperate struggle for survival, and it should not be attempted until the defects are remedied. Instead, and much simpler, enter the forest from the roadbridge over the Rede and proceed in comfort through it on a gravel road until, at a junction, a right turn leads down to the footbridge at Byrness (as shown on this map).

Blakehopeburnhaugh to Cottonshopeburn Foot:

What long names! Wainwright is bad enough, but these! An amendment proposed by the Northern Area (of course) is likely to be adopted and has been anticipated on this map. The route, hitherto passing through the forest and across a field direct to Cottonshopeburn Foot (beware bull), now keeps closely to the river bank (don't beware bull). Tall grass after initial good path.

Not as easy as it looks.

Brownrigg Head to the Border

The recommendations of the Northern Area of the Ramblers' Association

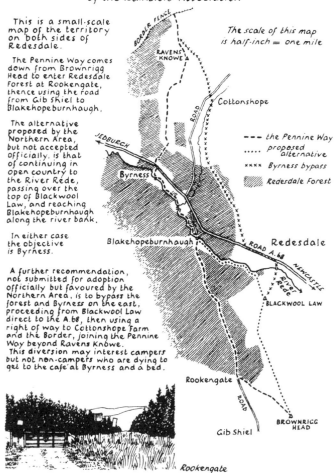

This is a small-scale map of the territory on both sides of Redesdale.

The Pennine Way comes down from Brownrigg Head to enter Redesdale Forest at Rookengate, thence using the road from Gib Shiel to Blakehopeburnhaugh.

The alternative proposed by the Northern Area, but not accepted officially, is that of continuing in open country to the River Rede, passing over the top of Blackwool Law, and reaching Blakehopeburnhaugh along the river bank.

In either case the objective is Byrness.

A further recommendation, not submitted for adoption officially but favoured by the Northern Area, is to bypass the forest and Byrness on the east, proceeding from Blackwool Law direct to the A.68, then using a right of way to Cottonshope Farm and the Border, joining the Pennine Way beyond Ravens Knowe. This diversion may interest campers but not non-campers who are dying to get to the café at Byrness and a bed.

The scale of this map is half-inch = one mile

BORDER FENCE

RAVENS KNOWE

Cottonshope

ROAD

JEDBURGH

Byrness

- - - the Pennine Way
..... proposed alternative
xxxx Byrness bypass
▨ Redesdale Forest

Blakehopeburnhaugh

ROAD A.68

Redesdale

NEWCASTLE

RIVER REDE

BLACKWOOL LAW

Rookengate

ROAD

Gib Shiel

BROWNRIGG HEAD

Rookengate

BROWNRIGG HEAD TO BLAKEHOPEBURNHAUGH

Landranger Sheet 80

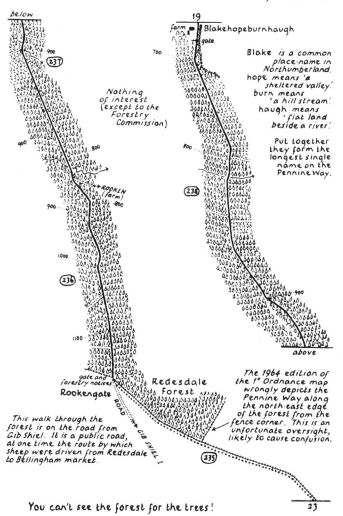

below

237

Nothing
of interest
(except to the
Forestry
Commission)

900

800

900

↘ROOKEN
(farm)

800

900

1000

236

1100

gate and
forestry notices

Rookengate

Redesdale
Forest

ROAD

GIB SHIEL !

235

This walk through the
forest is on the road from
Gib Shiel. It is a public road,
at one time the route by which
sheep were driven from Redesdale
to Bellingham market.

19

farm ■ Blakehopeburnhaugh

gate

700

Blake is a common
place·name in
Northumberland.
hope means 'a
sheltered valley'.
burn means
'a hill stream'.
haugh means
'flat land
beside a river'.

Put together
they form the
longest single
name on the
Pennine Way.

800

238

900

above

The 1964 edition of
the 1° Ordnance map
wrongly depicts the
Pennine Way along
the north·east edge
of the forest from the
fence corner. This is an
unfortunate oversight,
likely to cause confusion.

You can't see the forest for the trees!

23

The Brownrigg Head diversion

The members of the Northern Area of the Ramblers' Association take pride in the fact that much of the Pennine Way lies within their 'home' territory, and have been active in suggesting certain improvements to the original official line of the route for some miles on both sides of Redesdale, of which they did not, and still do not, fully approve, their argument being that a better course is available on existing rights of way that would obviate a long section of road-walking and forest-walking and keep to the open country instead. Their representations have, in part, succeeded, resulting in the new diversion over Padon Hill and Brownrigg Head, in lieu of the road walk to Gib Shiel, but they wanted also to have the route continued from Brownrigg Head to Blakehopeburnhaugh by way of Kelly's Pike, Blackwool Law, Dead Wood and the southern bank of the River Rede. This latter alternative, however, has been rejected, and the official route, at the time of writing, follows the fence from Brownrigg Head to Rookengate and there joins the road from Gib Shiel for the descent to Blakehopeburnhaugh through the forest, as indicated in this book.

The monument on Padon Hill

GIB SHIEL ROAD TO BROWNRIGG HEAD

Landranger Sheet 80

21

heather and grass

direction of BLACKWOOL LAW (see note opposite)

Brownrigg Head 1191' (234)

1100

It may be noted that Padon Hill is slightly more elevated than Winshields Crag (1230') on the Roman Wall and is therefore the highest point since Cross Fell. As its excellent view indicates, however, much higher ground lies ahead, across Redesdale: the Cheviots.

Brownrigg Head, an upland desert, is without charm; a place to vacate quickly for more pleasant scenes. It is remarkable only for its many boundary stones

bracken
1000

plantation

grass

GIB SHIEL ← gateway

hurdle

The 'pepperbox' monument on Padon Hill is slightly off-route, but is worthy of the small detour. Probably solid stonework throughout, or with a core of rubble (there is no entrance), it stands fifteen feet high amongst a scattering of stones, which appear to be the mason's discards. It seems unlikely that the stones, used or not used, are native to the hilltop — all around is undisturbed turf or heather, and therefore only by human effort can their presence on this remote summit be accounted for. There is a rough inscription, carved on a tablet, over which the inevitable initials of visitors are superimposed — its message cannot now be deciphered with certainty. The monument commemorates one Alexander Padon, a Scottish Covenanter who held religious meetings here, far from the long arm of persecution, and, according to legend, every worshipper was required to bring one stone. Those were the days!

If the monument is visited, easier walking will be found down the east side of the fence, instead of immediately rejoining the official route on the west side, which encounters thick heather.

1000 heather

heather

1100

(233)

heather

Padon Hill 1240 × monument

top wire of fence omitted for access to the monument

1200

heather

1180

fence renewed recently: beware loose wire

heather and grass

1100 hurdle △

Cross the road, not the cattle grid, and continue by the fence. The section of the route on this page is safe in mist, the fence (or, in one place, on the rise to Brownrigg Head, a wall) being continuously alongside.

Only one item of interest

big boulder △ cattle grid

(232) ROAD TROUGHEND 3

GIB SHIEL 2 BYRNESS 8½ 25

Summit of Lord's Shaw

Summit of Deer Play

Summit of Lough Shaw

HARESHAW COLLIERY TO GIB SHIEL ROAD

Landranger Sheet 80

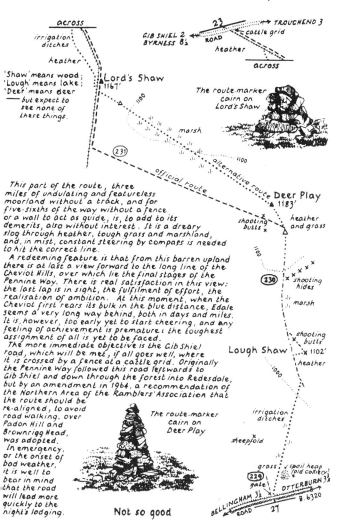

across

irrigation ditches

heather

'Shaw' means wood;
'Lough' means lake;
'Deer' means deer
— but expect to
see none of
these things.

23 → TROUCHEND 3

GIB SHIEL 2
BYRNESS 8½ ← ROAD → cattle grid

heather

across

▲ Lord's Shaw
1167'

1100

marsh

1100

The route-marker
cairn on
Lord's Shaw

(231)

official route

alternative route

Deer Play
▲ 1183'

shooting
butts

heather
and grass

1100

(230)

shooting
hides

marsh

shooting
butts

Lough Shaw

x 1102'

heather

1000

irrigation
ditches

sheepfold

grass

spoil heap
(old colliery)

(229)

gate

OTTERBURN 3½

BELLINGHAM 3½
ROAD

B.6320

27

This part of the route, three
miles of undulating and featureless
moorland without a track, and for
five-sixths of the way without a fence
or a wall to act as guide, is, to add to its
demerits, also without interest. It is a dreary
slog through heather, tough grass and marshland,
and, in mist, constant steering by compass is needed
to hit the correct line.

A redeeming feature is that from this barren upland
there is at last a view forward to the long line of the
Cheviot Hills, over which lie the final stages of the
Pennine Way. There is real satisfaction in this view:
the last lap is in sight, the fulfilment of effort, the
realisation of ambition. At this moment, when the
Cheviot first rears its bulk in the blue distance, Edale
seems a very long way behind, both in days and miles.
It is, however, too early yet to start cheering, and any
feeling of achievement is premature: the toughest
assignment of all is yet to be faced.

The more immediate objective is the Gib Shiel
road, which will be met, if all goes well, where
it is crossed by a fence at a cattle grid. Originally
the Pennine Way followed this road leftwards to
Gib Shiel and down through the forest into Redesdale,
but by an amendment in 1964, a recommendation of
the Northern Area of the Ramblers' Association that
the route should be
re-aligned, to avoid
road walking, over
Padon Hill and
Brownrigg Head,
was adopted.
In emergency,
or the onset of
bad weather,
it is well to
bear in mind
that the road
will lead more
quickly to the
night's lodging.

The route-marker
cairn on
Deer Play

Not so good

Map revised 1994.

Hareshaw

Blakelaw

Hareshaw Linn

BELLINGHAM TO HARESHAW COLLIERY

Landranger Sheet 80

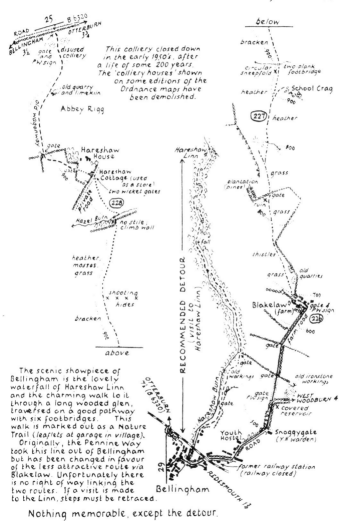

This colliery closed down in the early 1950's, after a life of some 200 years. The 'colliery houses' shown on some editions of the Ordnance maps have been demolished.

The scenic showpiece of Bellingham is the lovely waterfall of Hareshaw Linn and the charming walk to it through a long wooded glen, traversed on a good pathway with six footbridges. This walk is marked out as a Nature Trail (leaflets at garage in village).

Originally, the Pennine Way took this line out of Bellingham but has been changed in favour of the less attractive route via Blakelaw. Unfortunately there is no right of way linking the two routes. If a visit is made to the Linn, steps must be retraced.

Nothing memorable, except the detour.

The River North Tyne
at Bellingham

Footbridge,
Houxty Burn.

Shitlington Crags

LINACRES ROAD TO BELLINGHAM

Landranger Sheets 86 and 80

Bellingham (pron Bellinjam),
a large village in pleasant
surroundings, is the 'capital'
of the North Tyne valley. It
has shops, hotels, buses and
a disused railway station, an
attractive waterfall nearby
and a fine river.
Accommodation is obtainable and
there is a Youth Hostel. It is the
last shopping centre on the route,
going north, and, with 45 miles
still to do, an obvious place for a
final stock-taking.

FALSTONE 8

OTTERBURN 7½

(to B6320)

225

River

North

Road

Bellingham

Northumberland
National Park
sign

KIELDER 17

Cemetery

School

Bus Service
(Bellingham -
Hexham)
ROAD B6320

224

Eals
(farm)

stile, gate
PW sign
and old notice

HEXHAM 16

400

500

gate

Beyond the crags
mentioned below, which
are easily ascended by a
distinct path, a rising
pasture leads on to an
excellent cart-track on
Ealingham Rigg. Follow
this eastwards to a PW sign,
strike across a rough pasture
with many confusing sheep-tracks,
and, with Bellingham at last in
sight in the valley ahead
to spur flagging footsteps,
enter it triumphantly along
the Hexham road.

stile

gate

600

ROAD

old ditch

Ealingham Rigg

heather
gate

gate
and
PW sign

bracken
too.

cart track

223

PW sign

across

At the T-junction of roads, leave them all and go ahead
through fields alongside a hedge, bearing left on the
descent to a footbridge over Houxty Burn and turning
right on the far bank to another footbridge across a
tributary, then left through a gate and up a road in
a cutting to Shitlington Hall (a name that sounds a
trifle earthy: why not a reversion to the former
Shotlyngton Hall?). However, it is no business of
ours, so keep to the right around this place
into a hollow, then uphill through fields to the
similarly-tainted form of Shitlington Crag (most
easily by-passed on the right) and up to a low line
of crags with the same name (don't want to keep on
writing it), which provide a welcome change of scene.

across

Shitlington
Crags

gate

Shitlington
Crag (farm)

gateway

500

222

gate

gate

ROAD

Shitlington
Hall (farm)

400

gate
footbridge

Soot Burn

footbridge

600

HOUXTY
BURN

gateway

gateway
gate

500

500

221

ROAD

ROAD

MARK 2½

500

31

Cross-country rambling.

Low Stead

Hawthorn blossom in the
valley of Warks Burn

WARK FOREST (CENTRAL) TO LINACRES ROAD

Landranger Sheet 86

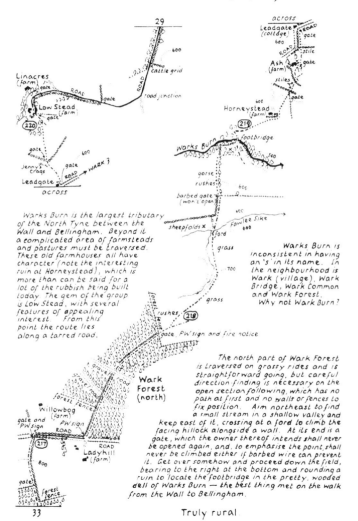

across
Leadgate
(cottage)   ROAD
600   gate
Ash
(farm)   gate
             stiles   stile
                           gate
Horneystead   600
(farm)
220

Works Burn   footbridge
              600

gorse
rushes   600
barbed gate
(won't open)
sheepfolds ×   Fawlee Sike
                ford   600
                grass   700

grass

29
600
cattle grid
ROAD
road junction

Linacres
(farm)   gate
          ROAD   gate
Low Stead
(farm)   gate
220

gate   600
Jenny's
Crags   gate   WARK 3
Leadgate ROAD
across

Warks Burn is the largest tributary
of the North Tyne between the
Wall and Bellingham. Beyond it
a complicated area of farmsteads
and pastures must be traversed.
These old farmhouses all have
character (note the interesting
ruin at Horneystead), which is
more than can be said for a
lot of the rubbish being built
today. The gem of the group
is Low Stead, with several
features of appealing
interest. From this
point the route lies
along a tarred road.

Warks Burn is
inconsistent in having
an 's in its name. In
the neighbourhood is
Wark (village), Wark
Bridge, Wark Common
and Wark Forest.
Why not Wark Burn?

rushes   218
gate, PW sign and fire notice

grass

gravel
forest fence

Wark
Forest
(north)

Willowbog
(farm)
gate and   PW sign
PW sign   ROAD
217
800   Ladyhill
            (farm)

gate
       forest
       fence
33

The north part of Wark Forest
is traversed on grassy rides and is
straightforward going, but careful
direction-finding is necessary on the
open section following, which has no
path at first and no walls or fences to
fix position. Aim northeast to find
a small stream in a shallow valley and
keep east of it, crossing at a ford to climb the
facing hillock alongside a wall. At its end is a
gate, which the owner thereof intends shall never
be opened again, and, to emphasise the point shall
never be climbed either if barbed wire can prevent
it. Get over somehow and proceed down the field,
bearing to the right at the bottom and rounding a
ruin to locate the footbridge in the pretty, wooded
dell of Warks Burn — the best thing met on the walk
from the Wall to Bellingham.

Truly rural.

The Border Forests

The Border Forest Park, established in 1955, is the largest of Britain's planted forests, and yet probably the least known because of its remoteness from centres of population and tourist routes. It occupies a vast tract of reclaimed heath on both sides of the Scottish Border, extending, with other adjacent forests outside the Park boundary, over an area of nearly 300 square miles, formerly largely an uncultivated wilderness with a few isolated habitations and a sparse and declining population : an upland desert, a wasteland.

Very different is the picture today.   For mile after mile these rolling moors have sprouted a mantle of growing timber, mainly the hardy Sitka spruce, with open areas left for husbandry and sheepfarming. Within the forests new villages have been created for the men who construct the roads, plant and maintain the crop, and will reap the ultimate harvest — after a wait of some 40 years.

The coming of the forests has brought life and prosperity to a district that was dying of poverty, hope where there was no hope. The transformation is complete.

The Park is formed by six principal forests:

      KIELDER
      WARK
      REDESDALE
      KERSHOPE
      NEWCASTLETON
      WAUCHOPE

The Pennine Way skirts the eastern fringe of the group, actually entering and passing through the Wark and Redesdale Forests for a few miles on gravel roads or rides (fire breaks).

'Border Guide', a National Forest Guide published by H.M. Stationery Office (5/-) is a well-written and fascinating account of the history, legend, flora and fauna, etc.
'A Short Guide to the Border Forest Park' is also published at 6d.

WAUCHOPE

REDESDALE

KIELDER

NEWCASTLETON

KERSHOPE

WARK

TEN MILES

Border : ·················
Pennine Way : - - - - - -

WARK FOREST (SOUTH) TO WARK FOREST (CENTRAL)

Landranger Sheet 86

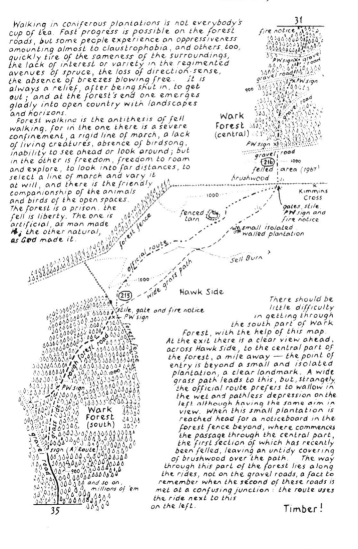

Walking in coniferous plantations is not everybody's cup of tea. Fast progress is possible on the forest roads, but some people experience an oppressiveness amounting almost to claustrophobia, and others too, quickly tire of the sameness of the surroundings, the lack of interest or variety in the regimented avenues of spruce, the loss of direction-sense, the absence of breezes blowing free. It is always a relief, after being shut in, to get out; and at the forest's end one emerges gladly into open country with landscapes and horizons.

Forest walking is the antithesis of fell walking, for in the one there is a severe confinement, a rigid line of march, a lack of living creatures, absence of birdsong, inability to see ahead or look around; but in the other is freedom, freedom to roam and explore, to look into far distances, to select a line of march and vary it at will, and there is the friendly companionship of the animals and birds of the open spaces. The fell is liberty. The one is artificial, as man made it; the other natural, as God made it.

There should be little difficulty in getting through the south part of Wark Forest, with the help of this map. At the exit there is a clear view ahead, across Hawk Side, to the central part of the forest, a mile away — the point of entry is beyond a small and isolated plantation, a clear landmark. A wide grass path leads to this, but, strangely, the official route prefers to wallow in the wet and pathless depression on the left although having the same aim in view. When this small plantation is reached head for a noticeboard in the forest fence beyond, where commences the passage through the central part, the first section of which has recently been felled, leaving an untidy covering of brushwood over the path. The way through this part of the forest lies along the rides, not on the gravel roads, a fact to remember when the second of these roads is met at a confusing junction: the route uses the ride next to this on the left.

Timber!

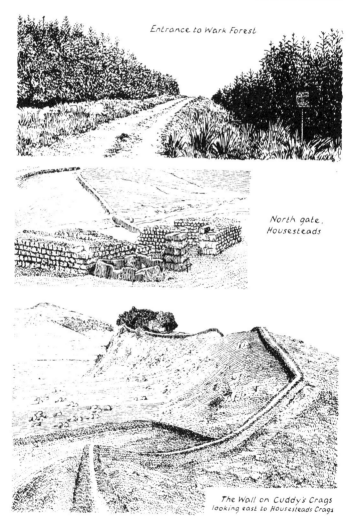

Entrance to Wark Forest

North gate,
Housesteads

The Wall on Cuddy's Crags
looking east to Housesteads Crags

RAPISHAW GAP TO WARK FOREST (SOUTH)

Landranger Sheet 86

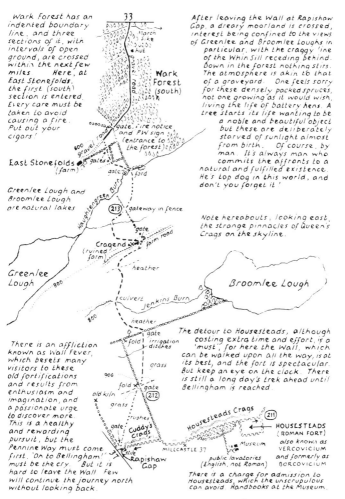

Wark Forest has an indented boundary line, and three sections of it, with intervals of open ground, are crossed within the next few miles. Here, at East Stonefolds, the first (south) section is entered. Every care must be taken to avoid causing a fire. Put out your cigars!

East Stonefolds (farm)

Greenlee Lough and Broomlee Lough are natural lakes

Greenlee Lough

After leaving the Wall at Rapishaw Gap, a dreary moorland is crossed, interest being confined to the views of Greenlee and Broomlee Loughs in particular, with the craggy line of the Whin Sill receding behind. Down in the forest nothing stirs. The atmosphere is akin to that of a graveyard. One feels sorry for these densely packed spruces, not one growing as it would wish, living the life of battery hens. A tree starts its life wanting to be a noble and beautiful object but these are deliberately starved of sunlight almost from birth. Of course, by man. It's always man who commits the affronts to a natural and fulfilled existence. He's top dog in this world, and don't you forget it!

Note hereabouts, looking east, the strange pinnacles of Queen's Crags on the skyline.

Broomlee Lough

There is an affliction known as Wall Fever, which besets many visitors to these old fortifications and results from enthusiasm and imagination, and a passionate urge to discover more. This is a healthy and rewarding pursuit, but the Pennine Way must come first. 'On to Bellingham!' must be the cry. But it is hard to leave the Wall. Few will continue the journey north without looking back.

The detour to Housesteads, although costing extra time and effort, is a 'must', for here the Wall, which can be walked upon all the way, is at its best, and the fort is spectacular. But keep an eye on the clock. There is still a long day's trek ahead until Bellingham is reached.

HOUSESTEADS (ROMAN FORT) also known as VERCOVICIUM and formerly as BORCOVICIUM

There is a charge for admission to Housesteads, which the unscrupulous can avoid. Handbooks at the Museum.

public lavatories (English, not Roman)

Farewell, Hadrian! Good show!

Dolerite pinnacles, Highshield Crag

Rapishaw Gap. This is the place at which the Pennine Way leaves the Wall to resume its journey northwards. Across the Gap the Wall is seen continuing over Cuddy's Crag. In the distance are Sewingshields Crag and Broomlee Lough.

Milecastle 39

Milecasties served as barracks for the soldiers on sentry duty in the turrets. Each milecastle had its north and south gates and an observation tower. Of the few remaining, No. 39 is one of the best-preserved.

The top of Winshields Crag
— the best viewpoint on the Wall; a place of vast skyscapes and sweeping landscapes. If visibility is good both the Solway and the North Sea will be seen in the wide panorama

The path on the Wall near Peel Crags

CAWFIELD CRAGS TO RAPISHAW GAP

Landranger Sheet 86

Some lengths of the Wall are sufficiently wide and soundly-based to permit walking along the top, distinct paths having been formed thereon by its 20th century legions (of visitors), and this is the common practice. These sections are indicated on the maps by arrows (← →), the usual symbol for a distinct path (------) being omitted for the sake of clarity.

Peel Crags and Highshield Crag are the two best-known rock-climbing grounds in Northumberland, their near-vertical walls of dolerite having yielded a hundred routes of varying degrees of difficulty.

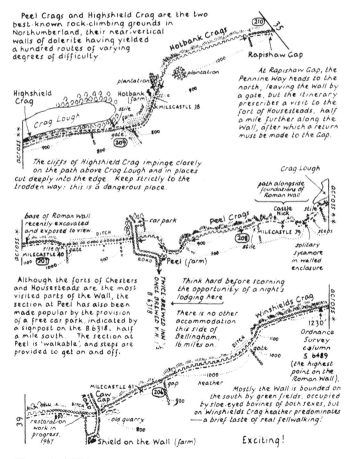

At Rapishaw Gap, the Pennine Way heads to the north, leaving the Wall by a gate, but the itinerary prescribes a visit to the fort of Housesteads, half a mile further along the Wall, after which a return must be made to the Gap.

The cliffs of Highshield Crag impinge closely on the path above Crag Lough and in places cut deeply into the edge. Keep strictly to the trodden way: this is a dangerous place.

base of Roman Wall recently excavated and exposed to view

Although the forts of Chesters and Housesteads are the most visited parts of the Wall, the section at Peel has also been made popular by the provision of a free car park, indicated by a signpost on the B6318, half a mile south. The section at Peel is 'walkable', and steps are provided to get on and off.

Think hard before scorning the opportunity of a night's lodging here

There is no other accommodation this side of Bellingham, 16 miles on.

Mostly the Wall is bounded on the south by green fields, occupied by sloe-eyed bovines of both sexes, but on Winshields Crag heather predominates — a brief taste of real fellwalking!

Exciting!

Map revised 1994.

Turret 44B

Milecastles were built adjoining the south side of the Wall at intervals of one Roman mile (1620 yds) and between them two turrets were erected, abutting on the Wall also and spaced at equal distances, for use as lookout towers.   The numbering of the turrets and milecastles is modern (for identification) and is from east to west, Turret 44B following Turret 44A and Milecastle 44.   Many of the turrets have fallen into complete decay that illustrated above, with its walls diminished to 5 feet in height, being one of the best specimens remaining.

The Wall

The drawing shows the Wall crossing the depression in the ridge east of Walltown Quarry, where it is joined by the Pennine Way. This part has been repaired recently to arrest further decay The Wall here varies in height, from 2½ to 7½ feet (original height thought to be 15 feet) and is 7½ feet in width with plinth projections. This is a typical remnant although differences in constructional details are apparent in the various sections remaining extant along its length.

RLWALL CASTLE TO CAWFIELD CRAGS

Landranger Sheet 86

The symbol used throughout this book to indicate a stone wall is a line of small circles, thus: ∞∞∞∞∞∞∞∞∞   The Roman Wall, however, is a very special wall, meriting a distinctive symbol, and is indicated thus: ⌐ⁿⁿⁿⁿⁿⁿⁿ , but only where it occurs in its original (now ruinous) state. In those places where it has been demolished to ground level and substituted by an ordinary stone wall of normal dimensions, with or without the incorporation of Roman stones found on the site, the usual symbol is used: ∞∞∞∞∞∞∞∞   (see also the note at the top of page 37)

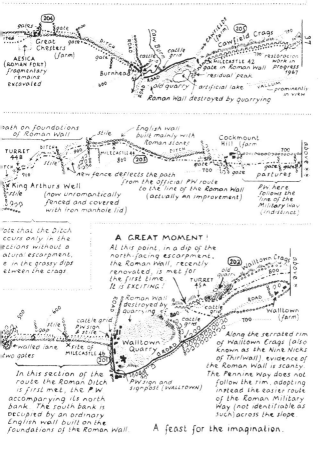

A GREAT MOMENT!
At this point, in a dip of the north-facing escarpment, the Roman Wall, recently renovated, is met for the first time. It is EXCITING!

Note that the Ditch occurs only in the sections without a natural escarpment, i.e. in the grassy dips between the crags.

In this section of the route the Roman Ditch is first met, the PW accompanying its north bank. The south bank is occupied by an ordinary English wall built on the foundations of the Roman Wall.

Along the serrated rim of Walltown Crags (also known as the Nine Nicks of Thirlwall), evidence of the Roman Wall is scanty. The Pennine Way does not follow the rim, adopting instead the easier route of the Roman Military Way (not identifiable as such) across the slope.

A feast for the imagination.

Thirlwall Castle

The Roman Wall

Drooping spirits on the weary trudge across the wastelands of Wain Rigg and Black Hill can be stimulated to some extent by licking parched lips over the early prospect of arrival in terrain of greater interest — the Wall Country, where profuse evidences of Roman military occupation are still clearly to be seen, together forming a most remarkable monument to the activities of those early conquerors. Here at last is the Roman Wall and its ramifications (also known, more correctly, as Hadrian's Wall, after the emperor who inspired it). Happily, the route of the Pennine Way coincides with the best-preserved parts of the fortifications.

What is to be seen will be appreciated more fully, and understood better, if information on the subject has been studied in advance. Of the many books available, the most useful for the casual visitor is "A Short Guide to the Roman Wall" by R.G. Collingwood, M.A., F.S.A. (Andrew Reid & Co. Ltd, Newcastle) although this has the slight disadvantage for Pennine Way walkers travelling to the Border of describing the Wall in the converse direction, from east to west.

Coming down from Black Hill, a serrated line of crags, like a succession of breaking waves, will be seen stretching into the distance eastwards — the Whin Sill, a hard basaltic formation known also as dolerite (remember it in upper Teesdale?). Along this crest, defended from the north by the natural steep fall of the rocks, and in the hollows between by a manmade ditch, is the Roman Wall with its regularly-spaced milecastles and turrets, and its occasional forts linked by a military way, the whole system being bounded on the south by an elaborate channel known as the vallum.

All these relics of the distant past will be seen. The Wall has immense appeal to the imagination, and its elevation and situation, overlooking a vast landscape, commands all approaches, as its builders intended.

So cheer up. Tomorrow will be more exciting than today.

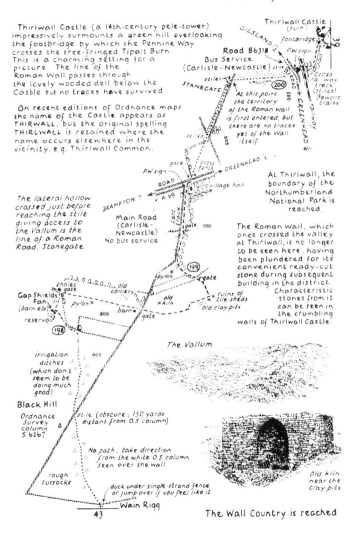

Thirlwall Castle (a 14th-century pele-tower) impressively surmounts a green hill overlooking the footbridge by which the Pennine Way crosses the tree-fringed Tipalt Burn. This is a charming setting for a picture. The line of the Roman Wall passes through the lovely wooded dell below the Castle but no traces have survived.

On recent editions of Ordnance maps the name of the Castle appears as THIRLWALL, but the original spelling THIRLWALL is retained where the name occurs elsewhere in the vicinity, e.g. Thirlwall Common.

The lateral hollow crossed just before reaching the stile giving access to the Vallum is the line of a Roman Road, Stanegate.

At this point the territory of the Roman Wall is first entered, but there are no traces yet of the Wall itself

At Thirlwall, the boundary of the Northumberland National Park is reached.

The Roman Wall, which once crossed the valley at Thirlwall, is no longer to be seen here, having been plundered for its convenient ready-cut stone during subsequent building in the district. Characteristic stones from it can be seen in the crumbling walls of Thirlwall Castle.

Thirlwall Castle (ruin)
footbridge
PW sign
Road B6318
Bus Service
(Carlisle-Newcastle)
stile
GILSLAND
Cross railway track (stiles) Beware trains
STANEGATE
VALLUM 200
GREENHEAD
railway
stiles
stiles
gate
cross fence
PW sign
ROAD
GREENHEAD
village hall
BRAMPTON
A 69
Main Road
(Carlisle-Newcastle)
No bus service
cart track
gate 700
199
gate
pylon
chalet gate
old colliery
Gap Shields Farm
(barn etc.)
pylon
barn gate
old kiln
ruins of lile sheds
old clay pits
reservoir
198
irrigation ditches (which don't seem to be doing much good)
900
Black Hill
Ordnance Survey column S. 6267
stile (obscure; 150 yards distant from O.S. column)
No path, take direction from the white O.S. column seen over the wall
rough tussocks
duck under single-strand fence or jump over if you feel like it
43
Wain Rigg

The Vallum

Old kiln near the clay pits

The Wall Country is reached

Hartley Burn

Footbridge over Kellah Burn,
looking to Greenriggs

Derelict cottage and air shaft,
Lambley Colliery

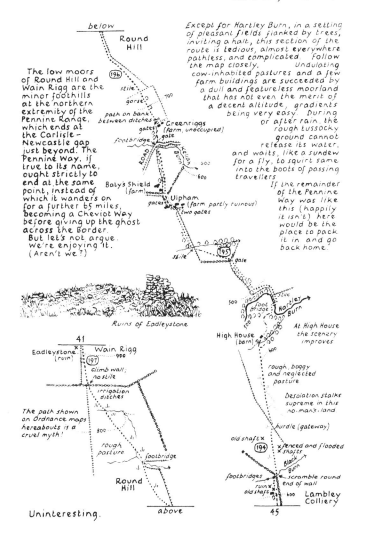

below

Round Hill

(196)

stile

gorse 700

path on bank between ditches

Greenriggs (farm, unoccupied)

gates

gate

footbridge

Kellah Burn

500

600

Baty's Shield (farm)

Ulpham (farm partly ruinous)

gates

two gates

stile

(195)

gate

Ruins of Eadleystone

500

foot bridge

Hartley Burn

High House (barn)

600

41

Eadleystone (ruin)

Wain Rigg 900

(197)

climb wall; no stile

irrigation ditches

800

rough pasture

footbridge

Round Hill

above

At High House the scenery improves

rough, boggy and neglected pasture

Desolation stalks supreme in this no-man's-land

hurdle (gateway)

old shaft ×

(194)

× fenced and flooded shafts

Black Burn

footbridges

scramble round end of wall

ruin
old shaft

600

Lambley Colliery

45

The low moors of Round Hill and Wain Rigg are the minor foothills at the northern extremity of the Pennine Range, which ends at the Carlisle–Newcastle gap just beyond. The Pennine Way, if true to its name, ought strictly to end at the same point, instead of which it wanders on for a further 65 miles, becoming a Cheviot Way before giving up the ghost across the Border.
But let's not argue. We're enjoying it. (Aren't we?)

Except for Hartley Burn, in a setting of pleasant fields flanked by trees, inviting a halt, this section of the route is tedious, almost everywhere pathless, and complicated. Follow the map closely. Undulating cow-inhabited pastures and a few farm buildings are succeeded by a dull and featureless moorland that has not even the merit of a decent altitude, gradients being very easy. During or after rain, the rough tussocky ground cannot release its water, and waits, like a sundew for a fly, to squirt same into the boots of passing travellers.
If the remainder of the Pennine Way was like this (happily it isn't) here would be the place to pack it in and go back home!

The path shown on Ordnance maps hereabouts is a cruel myth!

Uninteresting.

The Maiden Way
near Lambley

Glendue Bridge

Burnstones

SLAGGYFORD TO LAMBLEY COLLIERY

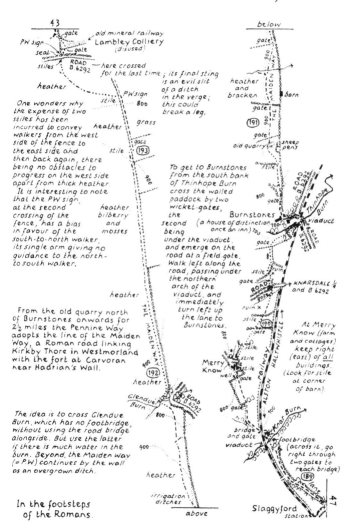

old mineral railway
Lambley Colliery
(disused)

43

gate
PW sign
seat
gate
stiles
ROAD — here crossed
B 6292   for the last time; its final sting
is an evil slit
of a ditch
in the verge;
this could
break a leg.

heather

PW sign
stile
800

grass

One wonders why
the expense of two
stiles has been
incurred to convey
walkers from the west
side of the fence to
the east side and
then back again, there
being no obstacles to
progress on the west side
apart from thick heather.
 It is interesting to note
that the PW sign,
at the second   heather
crossing of the   bilberry
fence, has a bias   and
in favour of the   mosses
south-to-north walker,
its single arm giving no
guidance to the north-
to south walker.

heather

gate
stile
(193)

900

From the old quarry north
of Burnstones onwards for
2½ miles the Pennine Way
adopts the line of the Maiden
Way, a Roman road linking
Kirkby Thore in Westmorland
with the fort at Carvoran
near Hadrian's Wall.

heather

THE MAIDEN

(192)

900

Glendue
Burn

ROAD
B 6292

800

The idea is to cross Glendue
Burn, which has no footbridge,
without using the road bridge
alongside. But use the latter
if there is much water in the
burn. Beyond, the Maiden Way
(= P.W.) continues by the wall
as an overgrown ditch.

900

heather

irrigation
ditches

In the footsteps
of the Romans.

above

below

gate

THE MAIDEN

heather
and
bracken

barn

gate

(191)

gate
old quarry   sheep
pens

stile

800

To get to Burnstones
from the south bank
of Thinhope Burn
cross the walled
paddock by two
wicket-gates,
the
second   Burnstones
being   (a house of distinction
under the viaduct,   once an inn) 700
and emerge on the
road at a field-gate.
Walk left along the
road, passing under
the northern
arch of the
viaduct, and
immediately
turn left up
the lane to
Burnstones.

ROAD
B 6292

Thinhope
Burn

viaduct

gate

stile
gate

ruin

KNARSDALE ¼
and B 6292

ROAD

ruin ×

stile

(190)

gate

At Merry
Know (farm
and cottages)
keep right
(east) of all
buildings.
(Look for stile
at corner
of barn).

stile

stile

Merry
Know

stile
gate
well

RAILWAY   HALTWHISTLE   ALSTON

800 gate

bridge
and gate
viaduct

Knar Burn

footbridge
(across it, go
right through
two gates to
reach bridge)

(189)

gate

Slaggyford
station

47

Slaggyford

The River South Tyne, near Slaggyford

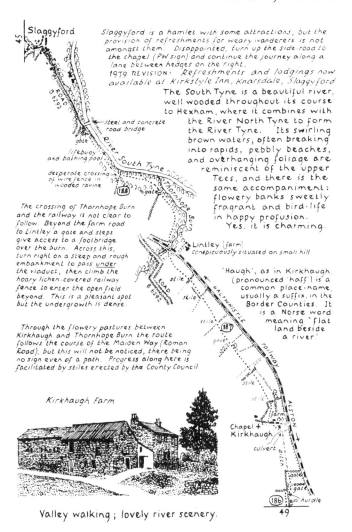

Slaggyford

Slaggyford is a hamlet with some attractions, but the provision of refreshments for weary wanderers is not amongst them. Disappointed, turn up the side-road to the chapel (PW sign) and continue the journey along a lane between hedges on the right.
1979 REVISION: *Refreshments and lodgings now available at Kirkstyle Inn, Knarsdale, Slaggyford*

The South Tyne is a beautiful river, well wooded throughout its course to Hexham, where it combines with the River North Tyne to form the River Tyne. Its swirling brown waters, often breaking into rapids, pebbly beaches, and overhanging foliage are reminiscent of the upper Tees, and there is the same accompaniment: flowery banks sweetly fragrant and bird-life in happy profusion. Yes, it is charming.

steel and concrete road bridge

gate

lifebuoy and bathing pool

desperate crossing of wire fence in wooded ravine

gate

River South Tyne

Thornhope Burn

The crossing of Thornhope Burn and the railway is not clear to follow. Beyond the farm road to Lintley a gate and steps give access to a footbridge over the burn. Across this, turn right on a steep and rough embankment to pass *under* the viaduct, then climb the hoary lichen-covered railway fence to enter the open field beyond. This is a pleasant spot but the undergrowth is dense.

Lintley (farm) conspicuously situated on small hill

stile

stile

stile

gate

'Haugh', as in Kirkhaugh (pronounced 'haff') is a common place-name, usually a suffix, in the Border Counties. It is a Norse word meaning 'flat land beside a river'

Through the flowery pastures between Kirkhaugh and Thornhope Burn the route follows the course of the Maiden Way (Roman Road), but this will not be noticed, there being no sign even of a path. Progress along here is facilitated by stiles erected by the County Council

HALTWHISTLE ROAD B 6292

railway ALSTON

Kirkhaugh Farm

Chapel Kirkhaugh

culvert

gate
gate
hurdle

Valley walking; lovely river scenery.

49

Alston

Alston
Bridge

49

ALSTON TO DYKE HOUSE

Landranger Sheet 86

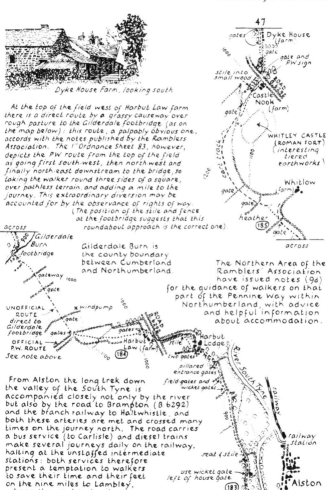

Dyke House Farm, looking south

At the top of the field west of Harbut Law farm there is a direct route by a grassy causeway over rough pasture to the Gilderdale footbridge (as on the map below): this route, a palpably obvious one, accords with the notes published by the Ramblers Association. The 1" Ordnance Sheet 83, however, depicts the PW route from the top of the field as going first south-west, then north-west and finally north-east downstream to the bridge, so taking the walker round three sides of a square, over pathless terrain, and adding a mile to the journey. This extraordinary diversion may be accounted for by the observance of rights of way.
(The position of the stile and fence at the footbridge suggests that this roundabout approach is the correct one).

Gilderdale Burn is the county boundary between Cumberland and Northumberland.

The Northern Area of the Ramblers' Association have issued notes (9d) for the guidance of walkers on that part of the Pennine Way within Northumberland, with advice and helpful information about accommodation.

UNOFFICIAL ROUTE direct to Gilderdale footbridge

OFFICIAL P.W. ROUTE See note above

From Alston the long trek down the valley of the South Tyne is accompanied closely not only by the river but also by the road to Brampton (B 6292) and the branch railway to Haltwhistle, and both these arteries are met and crossed many times on the journey north. The road carries a bus service (to Carlisle) and diesel trains make several journeys daily on the railway, halting at the unstaffed intermediate stations: both services therefore present a temptation to walkers to save their time and their feet on the nine miles to Lambley, where the road and railway part company with the Pennine Way.

Circuitous manœuvres to avoid road-walking.

51

Alston, formerly a lead-mining centre claiming to be the highest market town in England, has many noteworthy features.   To the walker on the Pennine Way the shops will be of more urgent interest than the picturesque and informal arrangement of its buildings and streets (how charming are the places unspoilt by town planning!), for Alston is the last opportunity of replenishing the rucksack this side of Bellingham, **42** miles on. Early closing day is Tuesday.   There is a railway station (terminus). Roads radiate from here in all directions, some with bus services. Although in Cumberland its affinities in the main are linked with the northeast.

The town itself is just off the route of the Pennine Way but few walkers are likely to pass it by on the other side unvisited.

Footbridge over the
River South Tyne

Garrigill

GARRIGILL TO ALSTON

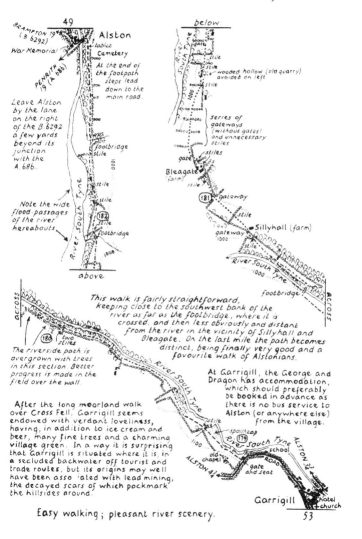

49

BRAMPTON 19 (B 6292)

War Memorial

Alston

tablet

Cemetery

PENRITH 19 (A 686)

At the end of the footpath steps lead down to the main road.

Leave Alston by the lane on the right of the B. 6292 a few yards beyond its junction with the A. 686.

River South Tyne

Note the wide flood-passages of the river hereabouts.

footbridge
stile

1001

stile

182

stile

footbridge

1000

above

below

South Tyne River

gate

stile

stile

wooded hollow (old quarry) avoided on left

stile

stile

series of gateways (without gates) and unnecessary stiles.

gate
stiles

Bleagate (farm)

stile

181 gateway

stile

Sillyhall (farm)

gateway
1000

stile

River South Tyne

1000

footbridge

Across

Across

186 two stiles

across

The riverside path is overgrown with trees in this section. Better progress is made in the field over the wall.

After the long moorland walk over Cross Fell, Garrigill seems endowed with verdant loveliness, having, in addition to ice cream and beer, many fine trees and a charming village green. In a way it is surprising that Garrigill is situated where it is, in a secluded backwater off tourist and trade routes, but its origins may well have been associated with lead mining, the decayed scars of which pockmark the hillsides around.

This walk is fairly straightforward, keeping close to the southwest bank of the river as far as the footbridge, where it is crossed, and then less obviously and distant from the river in the vicinity of Sillyhall and Bleagate. On the last mile the path becomes distinct, being finally very good and a favourite walk of Alstonians.

River South Tyne

At Garrigill, the George and Dragon has accommodation, which should preferably be booked in advance as there is no bus service to Alston (or anywhere else) from the village.

stile

spoilheap

ALSTON 4½

River South Tyne

1100

old chapel

ALSTON 4½

school

ALSTON 3½

gate and seat

ROAD

Garrigill

hotel
church

53

Easy walking; pleasant river scenery.

Lead Mining in the Pennines

The long descent to Garrigill is an exhilarating walk, with fine views ahead of the valley of the River South Tyne, where lies the next stage of the Pennine Way, but there is little of interest in the immediate vicinity after the Crossfell mines are left behind, and nothing worthy of illustration. The mines, however, may well have excited curiosity, and this page will therefore be devoted to a few additional notes on lead mining in the district. 338 pages on the subject, for those especially interested, will be found in a book, "A History of Lead Mining in the Pennines" by Dr. Arthur Raistrick, MSc and Bernard Jennings, MA, published by Longmans in 1965, which is not only an authoritative research but tells a fascinating story.

Lead mining is amongst the oldest of the Pennine industries. From chance finds in some of the mines and from excavations of their camps, it is known that the Romans worked in these hills for lead, and some evidence that they exploited surface mines opened and used by the native Britons earlier. These workings were not on a large scale, there being little domestic use for the mineral, but the industry subsequently developed considerably with the demand for lead as a roofing material in the building of the churches, abbeys, monasteries and castles throughout the country in the succeeding centuries. In later years, technical improvements assisted in the extraction and smelting processes, resulting in greater output to meet the growing demand for industrial purposes. The peak of activity was reached in the 19th century, but towards its end the cheaper supplies available from foreign sources caused so severe a check to home production that most of the Pennine mines became uneconomical to operate and were closed. Today they are derelict and abandoned, rotting monuments to an industry that perished.

In the Pennines the two main centres of mining activity were in the moorland area around Alston and in Swaledale and adjoining valleys. The Alston district was particularly rich in deposits, and mining became not only the main industry but a very important one, especially in the Nenthead and Allendale sectors, where the hills are scarred and defaced by old workings that mutely testify to the intense exploitation that brought a short-lived prosperity to this area. Today the landscape has the silence of desolation. Below the ground the lead is still there in quantity, waiting to be won.

The abandoned mines are of exceptional interest. Their past contribution to the social, economic and industrial life of many small Pennine communities is a valuable part of our history, our heritage. They are falling into irretrievable decay, except for a few still being worked for other minerals such as fluorspar and barytes. Is it too much to ask that the Ministry of Works, who undertake restoration and preservation so skilfully, or perhaps some enlightened local or public authority in the north, should acquire, restore and preserve a typical specimen lead mine as a site museum for the future benefit of engineering students or even the general public, who, if this is not done, will soon have lost for ever the opportunity to see how the enterprise, courage and skill of their countrymen long ago wrested a hard-earned living from these wild and inhospitable hills.

Yes, alas, it is too much to ask. Nothing will be done.

53

LONG MAN HILL TO GARRIGILL

Landranger Sheets 91 and 86

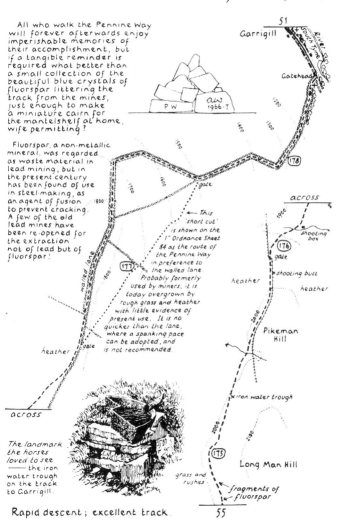

All who walk the Pennine Way will forever afterwards enjoy imperishable memories of their accomplishment, but if a tangible reminder is required what better than a small collection of the beautiful blue crystals of fluorspar littering the track from the mines, just enough to make a miniature cairn for the mantelshelf at home, wife permitting?

Fluorspar, a non-metallic mineral, was regarded as waste material in lead mining, but in the present century has been found of use in steel-making, as an agent of fusion to prevent cracking. A few of the old lead mines have been re-opened for the extraction not of lead but of fluorspar!

This 'short cut' is shown on the 1" Ordnance Sheet 84 as the route of the Pennine Way in preference to the walled lane. Probably formerly used by miners, it is today overgrown by rough grass and heather with little evidence of present use. It is no quicker than the lane, where a spanking pace can be adopted, and is not recommended.

The landmark the horses loved to see — the iron water trough on the track to Garrigill.

Rapid descent; excellent track.

Garrigill
Gateshead
51
178
177
176
175
across
shooting box
gate
shooting butt
heather
heather
Pikeman Hill
iron water trough
Long Man Hill
grass and rushes
fragments of fluorspar
across
heather
walled lane
gate
heather
55
River Tyne
South Tyne
P W   aw 1966·7

Relics of the old Mines on Cross Fell

A dry level (a main access to the mine, in some cases serviced by light railways for the extraction of ore and spoil)

Wet levels (conduits for draining water from the mine to the open hillside as an alternative to pumping, to prevent floods)

Ruined buildings.

The cottage illustrated (on the main route) has fireplaces and makes a good shelter and bivouac in emergency

An air shaft

A horse-drawn truck or sled

It is no discredit to the men who constructed these mines (their craftsmanship, even today, can be seen to be of the highest quality) to issue a warning to all explorers that they have become potentially dangerous. Nature, left alone, can do a lot of damage to man's creations in seventy years of man's neglect. Look at what is left on the surface, but keep out of the innards!

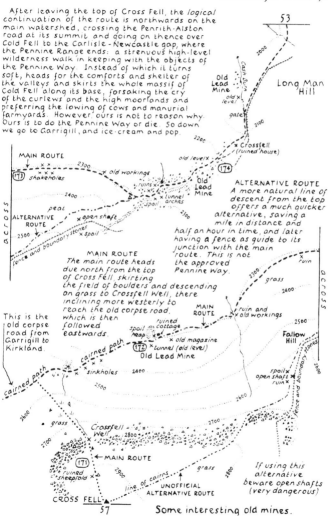

CROSS FELL TO LONG MAN HILL

Landranger Sheet 91

After leaving the top of Cross Fell, the *logical* continuation of the route is northwards on the main watershed, crossing the Penrith-Alston road at its summit and going on thence over Cold Fell to the Carlisle-Newcastle gap, where the Pennine Range ends: a strenuous high-level wilderness walk in keeping with the objects of the Pennine Way. Instead of which it turns soft, heads for the comforts and shelter of the valleys and skirts the whole massif of Cold Fell along its base, forsaking the cry of the curlews and the high moorlands and preferring the lowing of cows and manurial farmyards. However ours is not to reason why. Ours is to do the Pennine Way or die. So down we go to Garrigill, and ice-cream and pop.

53

Cash Burn

2000

Old Lead Mine
old x level

gate

2100

Long Man Hill

2200

x Crossfell (ruined house)

174

old level x

MAIN ROUTE
173
x x x shakeholes

2300

x old workings

x ruins x

2400

x tunnel arches

peat

Old Lead Mine

x old level x

spoil

2500

ALTERNATIVE ROUTE
x open shaft

x spoil

fence and boundary stones

2500

ALTERNATIVE ROUTE
A more natural line of descent from the top offers a much quicker alternative, saving a mile in distance and half an hour in time, and later having a fence as guide to its junction with the main route. This is not the approved Pennine Way.

2300
x ruin

grass

2400

MAIN ROUTE
The main route heads due north from the top of Cross Fell, skirting the field of boulders and descending on grass to Crossfell Well, there inclining more westerly to reach the old corpse road, which is then followed eastwards.

MAIN ROUTE
x ruin and x old workings

2500

Fallow Hill

2600

spoil x
open shaft
ruin x

This is the old corpse road from Garrigill to Kirkland.

cairned path

spoil heap

ruined cottage

MAIN ROUTE

x old magazine

172
x tunnel (old level)
Old Lead Mine

x x sinkholes

2400

2500

2600

fence and boundary stones

cairned path

2600

grass

x grass

Crossfell Well
2800

2700

line of cairns

2700

2900

171

x ruined sheepfold

MAIN ROUTE

2800

If using this alternative beware open shafts (very dangerous)

CROSS FELL
57

UNOFFICIAL ALTERNATIVE ROUTE

Some interesting old mines.

The 'ruined cottage' just beyond mile 172 is now Greg's Hut, a mountain refuge with bunks.

Cross Fell is the loftiest of the Pennines, and its summit, 2930', is the highest point reached on the Pennine Way. It is a giant, the top being a sprawling grassy plateau rimmed by a collar of scree and boulders, without paths and without landmarks — in mist navigation is difficult, confusion being worse confounded by a multiplicity of cairns, most of which serve no good purpose. As a viewpoint in clear weather, however, Cross Fell is second to none, its range extending from the peaks of Lakeland, superbly arrayed across the wide valley of the Eden, to the far extremes of the northern counties and into Scotland: a grand panorama. This bleak upland wilderness, a barrier between east and west, usually sullen and often ravaged by storm, is a meetingplace of turbulent air currents and the source of the fierce Helm Wind that so often scourges the valley along its western base.

In all respects, Cross Fell is a force to be reckoned with.

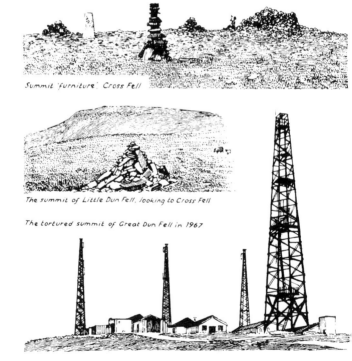

Summit 'furniture', Cross Fell

The summit of Little Dun Fell, looking to Cross Fell

The tortured summit of Great Dun Fell in 1967

Throughout the three miles mapped on this page the route lies along the main watershed at its greatest elevation. Here, east, are the headwaters of the Tees, and, west, feeders of the Eden. When Cross Fell is topped the vast drainage system of the Tyne is entered and not left until the Scottish Border is reached near the end of the journey.

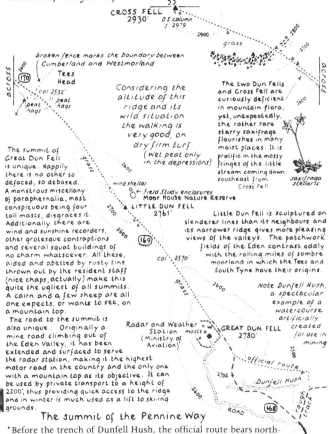

55

CROSS FELL
2930'
OS column
S 29.9

2900

grass

broken fence marks the boundary between Cumberland and Westmorland

170

Tees Head

col 2532'

peat hags

peat hags

The two Dun Fells and Cross Fell are curiously deficient in mountain flora, yet, unexpectedly, the rather rare starry saxifrage flourishes in many moist places. It is prolific in the mossy fringes of the little stream coming down southeast from Cross Fell.

saxifraga stellaris

Considering the altitude of this ridge and its wild situation the walking is very good, on dry firm turf (Wet peat only in the depressions)

The summit of Great Dun Fell is unique. Happily there is no other so defaced. A monstrous miscellany of paraphernalia, most conspicuous being four tall masts, disgraces it. Additionally there are wind and sunshine recorders, other grotesque contraptions and several squat buildings of no charm whatsoever. All these, aided and abetted by rusty tins thrown out by the resident staff (nice chaps, actually) make this quite the ugliest of all summits. A cairn and a few sheep are all one expects, or wants to see, on a mountain top.

The road to the summit is also unique. Originally a mine road climbing out of the Eden Valley, it has been extended and surfaced to serve the radar station, making it the highest motor road in the country and the only one with a mountain top as its objective. It can be used by private transport to a height of 2200', thus providing quick access to the ridge and in winter is much used as a lift to ski-ing grounds.

wind shelter

Field Study enclosures
Moor House Nature Reserve

LITTLE DUN FELL
2765'

Little Dun Fell is sculptured on slenderer lines than its neighbours and its narrower ridge gives more pleasing views of the valleys. The patchwork fields of the Eden contrast oddly with the rolling miles of sombre moorland in which the Tees and South Tyne have their origins.

169

col 2570'

Note Dunfell Hush, a spectacular example of a watercourse artificially created for use in mining.

Radar and Weather Station masts
(Ministry of Aviation)

GREAT DUN FELL
2780'

official route

Dunfell Hush

The summit of the Pennine Way

2700

ROAD

168

*Before the trench of Dunfell Hush, the official route bears north-east along a track, crosses the Hush and then bears west up to the radar station. However, because this route can be awkward during the winter, the alternative is to bear north-west, splitting the angle between the road and and the track, heading for the left edge of the radar station. Map revised 1994.

59

Cross Fell

Great Dun Fell

The summit of Knock Fell, looking northwest

Knock Old Man

Cairns on Knock Fell

Knock Hush

SWINDALE BECK TO GREAT DUN FELL

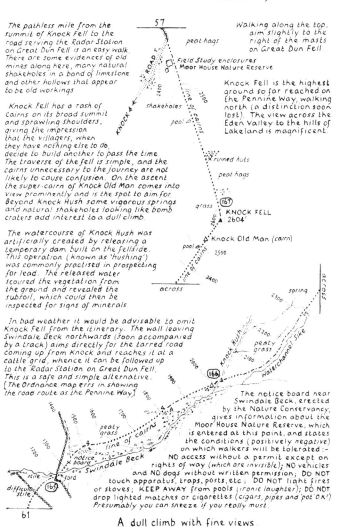

The pathless mile from the summit of Knock Fell to the road serving the Radar Station on Great Dun Fell is an easy walk. There are some evidences of old mines along here, many natural shakeholes in a band of limestone and other hollows that appear to be old workings.

Knock Fell has a rash of cairns on its broad summit and sprawling shoulders, giving the impression that the villagers, when they have nothing else to do, decide to build another to pass the time. The traverse of the fell is simple, and the cairns unnecessary to the journey are not likely to cause confusion. On the ascent the super-cairn of Knock Old Man comes into view prominently and is the spot to aim for. Beyond Knock Hush some vigorous springs and natural shakeholes looking like bomb craters add interest to a dull climb.

The watercourse of Knock Hush was artificially created by releasing a temporary dam built on the fellside. This operation (known as 'hushing') was commonly practised in prospecting for lead. The released water scoured the vegetation from the ground and revealed the subsoil, which could then be inspected for signs of minerals.

In bad weather it would be advisable to omit Knock Fell from the itinerary. The wall leaving Swindale Beck northwards (soon accompanied by a track) aims directly for the tarred road coming up from Knock and reaches it at a cattle grid, whence it can be followed up to the Radar Station on Great Dun Fell. This is a safe and simple alternative. [The Ordnance maps err in showing the road route as the Pennine Way.]

Walking along the top, aim slightly to the right of the masts on Great Dun Fell.

Knock Fell is the highest ground so far reached on the Pennine Way, walking north (a distinction soon lost). The view across the Eden Valley to the hills of Lakeland is magnificent.

The notice board near Swindale Beck, erected by the Nature Conservancy, gives information about the Moor House Nature Reserve, which is entered at this point, and states the conditions (positively negative) on which walkers will be tolerated :– NO access without a permit except on rights of way (which are invisible); NO vehicles and NO dogs without written permission; DO NOT touch apparatus, traps, posts, etc; DO NOT light fires or stoves; KEEP AWAY from pools (ironic laughter); DO NOT drop lighted matches or cigarettes (cigars, pipes and 'pot' O.K?) Presumably you can sneeze if you really must.

A dull climb with fine views

WESTMORLAND

*Footbridge
over
Great Rundale Beck*

*Dufton Pike
and the lane to Coatsike*

DUFTON TO SWINDALE BECK

Landranger Sheet 91

For half a mile beyond Coatsike the route follows a former access lane to the farm buildings of Halsteads (now used as a store). This was at one time a lovely flowery lane fringed with trees. The flowers and the trees are still there, but neglect has taken its toll and the lane has become wet and overgrown. Only walkers and an occasional tractor come this way now and they have formed a parallel path through the adjoining fields.

Beyond Halsteads the lane goes on, now unenclosed, to the ford across Great Rundale Beck and its quaint little clapper bridge. Here it may be noted how completely Dufton Pike is severed from the higher fells behind it by a side valley: a geographical curiosity that is repeated along this western base of the Pennines by Knock Pike and Murton Pike.

railway goods wagon

gate

Small Burn

Just beyond the railway container, where the path curves to the right, keep on straight ahead.

ford and footbridge

Great Rundale Beck

gate

Cosca Hill

Halsteads (farm)
(farmhouse unoccupied)

At Dufton there commences the highest part of the journey: the traverse of Cross Fell and its satellites, the loftiest ground in England outside the Lake District, with no accommodation until Garrigill is reached at the end of the day. Cross Fell is a surly beast, often in a black mood, and although the walk is nowhere arduous and route-finding is not really difficult, a fine day is to be desired if only to enjoy the finest view to be seen from the Pennine Way — the exciting skyline of Lakeland across the fertile Vale of Eden.

ruined barn

stile

tree and overgrown lane

barn

gate

The pleasant walk from Coatsike to Great Rundale Beck is dominated by the steep slope of Dufton Pike on the right, rising to a neat summit at 1578'. The surroundings are serene, quiet, peaceful. Cows graze contentedly in green fields. But the scenery in this part of Westmorland may change radically within a few years. The area is being suggested as a de-luxe sports centre on a mammoth scale, with a synthetic ski run, hotels and restaurants, covered swimming pools, huge car parks, and all the fun of the fair.

Some of us would prefer to see cows grazing contentedly in green fields.

Where the road to Knock bends left immediately beyond the junction of the Long Marton road keep straight ahead along the lane directly facing.

gates

Coatsike route (farm)

KNOCK

farm road

LONG MARTON 1½

Eller Beck

gooseberries are rampant in this lane

Youth hostellers overnight at Knock must return to this point if they wish to keep strictly to the official route of the Pennine Way.

Stag Inn
Dufton

A pleasant ramble.

*There is now a Youth Hostel in Dufton.

Dufton

High Cup

HIGH CUP TO DUFTON

Landranger Sheet 91

Dufton is a small cluster of neat cottages, with a school, a post office and an inn, around a village green embowered in trees: a typically charming Westmorland rural scene. Its homely friendliness is a complete contrast to the hostile and inhospitable wilderness of Maize Beck, and it is obviously the natural journey's end after the long crossing from Teesdale.

The height lost in descending to it from the watershed must be regained next morning, but nobody will regret an evening in lovely Dufton.

Youth-hostellers must however tramp two miles further, to the next village, Knock, to secure their night's lodging; and then retrace their steps next morning.

Non-youth-hostellers ought to bear in mind that accommodation in Dufton is too limited to cope with unheralded tourists arriving late and in quantity, and be prepared to tramp a further three miles to Appleby and three miles back in the morning.

Wise virgins book their beds in advance.

After all the sweat and toil and the many long miles of the march it is galling to note that Kirk Yetholm is further away at the end of the day than it was at the beginning!

From High Cup an improving path runs along the north edge of the escarpment and there is a good section at Narrow Gate where it traverses rock ledges sprayed by cascades. Then a line of cairns leads across the shoulder of the fell (leaving the valley of High Cup Gill, which descends to the large farm of Harbour Flatt, prominently seen) down into a green hollow delightfully decorated by limestone. Here an old kiln offers a useful hiding-place for anyone who wants to get out of sight for a minute. Then come the first stone walls since Birkdale and an excellent cart-track that leads to Bow Hall and becomes a tarred road to Dufton. Ahead, the Eden Valley and the fells of Lakeland form an inviting panorama.

Hannah's Well
— a spring beneath a boulder

A perfect end to the day

*There is now a Youth Hostel in Dufton.

The footbridge and the limestone gorge, Flood Route

The crevices and cracks in the limestone walls of this gorge nurture interesting specimens of wild flowers and mosses. Prominent is the handsome rose-root (*Sedum rosea*)

Narrowgate Beacon →

High Cup Nick

Nichol Chair

High Cup

High Cup is commonly referred to as High Cup Nick, which, however, is properly a cleft in the escarpment.

Nichol (or Nichol's) Chair (or Last)

This slender pillar of basalt (in view 20 yards from the path) is named after a Dufton cobbler who not only climbed it but, the story goes, soled and heeled a pair of boots whilst sitting on the top.

The split boulder where Maize Beck is rejoined

The ruins of Moss Shop

The cairn and spoil-heap at the Moss Shop mine

GRAIN BECK TO HIGH CUP

Landranger Sheet 91

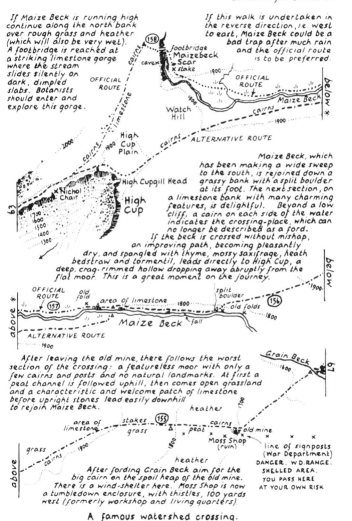

If Maize Beck is running high continue along the north bank over rough grass and heather (which will also be very wet). A footbridge is reached at a striking limestone gorge where the stream slides silently on dark, dimpled slabs. Botanists should enter and explore this gorge.

If this walk is undertaken in the reverse direction, i.e. west to east, Maize Beck could be a bad trap after much rain and the official route is to be preferred.

footbridge
Maizebeck Scar
cave
x stake

OFFICIAL ROUTE

OFFICIAL ROUTE

Maize Beck
cairns

Watch Hill

ALTERNATIVE ROUTE

High Cup Plain

cairns

limestone

High Cupgill Head

x Nichol Chair

High Cup

1700
1600
1500
1400
1300

Maize Beck, which has been making a wide sweep to the south, is rejoined down a grassy bank with a split boulder at its foot. The next section, on a limestone bank with many charming features, is delightful. Beyond a low cliff, a cairn on each side of the water indicates the crossing-place, which can no longer be described as a ford. If the beck is crossed without mishap, an improving path, becoming pleasantly dry, and spangled with thyme, mossy saxifrage, heath bedstraw and tormentil, leads directly to High Cup, a deep, crag-rimmed hollow dropping away abruptly from the flat moor. This is a great moment on the journey.

OFFICIAL ROUTE
old fold
area of limestone
split boulder
old folds

Maize Beck   *fall*

ALTERNATIVE ROUTE

After leaving the old mine, there follows the worst section of the crossing: a featureless moor with only a few cairns and posts and no natural landmarks. At first a peat channel is followed uphill, then comes open grassland and a characteristic and welcome patch of limestone before upright stones lead easily downhill to rejoin Maize Beck.

Grain Beck

area of limestone
stakes
cairns
old mine
grass
peat
Moss Shop (ruin)

heather

grass
cairns

heather

line of signposts (War Department)
DANGER. W.D. RANGE. SHELLED AREA. YOU PASS HERE AT YOUR OWN RISK

After fording Grain Beck aim for the big cairn on the spoil heap of the old mine. There is a wind-shelter here. Moss Shop is now a tumbledown enclosure, with thistles, 100 yards west (formerly workshop and living quarters).

A famous watershed crossing.

Top and middle maps amended 1994.

Cauldron
Snout

Cauldron Snout is a fine mountain cataract, but its impressiveness depends on its volume of water. After continuous heavy rain it is a tremendous spectacle, a torrent of angry, cascading waves, white with rage. Its rocky channel is dolerite.

The bridge

The final plunge

The loneliest inhabited place in Westmorland........

Birkdale,
looking east

Falcon Clints, looking east

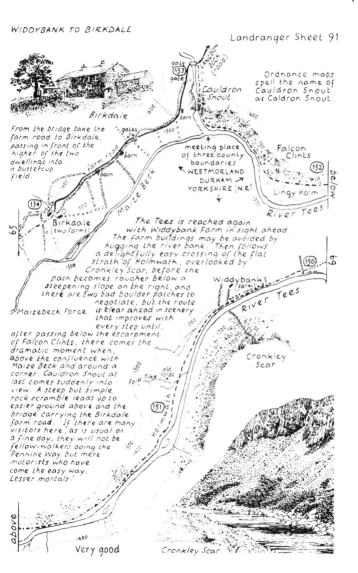

WIDDYBANK TO BIRKDALE

Landranger Sheet 91

Ordnance maps
spell the name of
Cauldron Snout
as Caldron Snout.

Birkdale

From the bridge take the
farm road to Birkdale,
passing in front of the
higher of the two
dwellings into
a buttercup
field.

gate
152
gate

LANGDON BECK (road)

Cauldron
Snout

Falcon
Clints

meeting place
of three county
boundaries
← WESTMORLAND
DURHAM →
YORKSHIRE (N.R.)

152

below

Lingy Holm

River Tees

134

Birkdale
(two farms)

Maize Beck

The Tees is reached again
with Widdybank Farm in sight ahead.
The farm buildings may be avoided by
hugging the river bank. Then follows
a delightfully easy crossing of the flat
strath of Holmwath, overlooked by
Cronkley Scar, before the
path becomes rougher below a
steepening slope on the right, and
there are two bad boulder patches to
negotiate, but the route
is clear ahead in scenery
that improves with
every step until,

150

Widdybank
farm

River Tees

Maizebeck Force

after passing below the escarpment
of Falcon Clints, there comes the
dramatic moment when,
above the confluence with
Maize Beck and around a
corner, Cauldron Snout at
last comes suddenly into
view. A steep but simple
rock scramble leads up to
easier ground above and the
bridge carrying the Birkdale
farm road. If there are many
visitors here, as is usual on
a fine day, they will not be
fellow-walkers doing the
Pennine Way but mere
motorists who have
come the easy way.
Lesser mortals!

Cronkley
Scar

old
folds

Fold Sike

151

Holm Sike

above

1400

Very good

Cronkley Scar

Conservation versus Destruction

The infant Tees, from its birth on Cross Fell, drains a wide area of rolling moorland that appears, at first sight, to be a desolate waste, a desert of peat and bog and heather, a no-man's land, a barren, hopeless wilderness. No region in the country, however, has yielded more valuable secrets to the searcher of scientific truths in those fields of inquiry dear to the naturalist. The geological interest is great, and the fauna is outstandingly rich and varied, but it is the remarkable flora of the district that has most firmly established its place amongst the most important areas of natural interest in Britain and as one especially worthy of conservation: it has, indeed, an international reputation and is regularly visited by scientists and students, while a permanent resident team conduct a continuous research.

This interest is shared by many who, seeking beauty rather than knowledge, simply love to wander in flowery pastures or alongside tumbling waters, and find pleasure in looking for the many kinds of plant life that are unique or exceedingly rare, not with any thought of wanton pillage but for true enjoyment.

It is against this background of amenity, scientific study and conservation, that proposals to establish reservoirs in upper Teesdale have excited and stimulated so much opposition in recent years. Most seriously under threat is the shallow basin of Cow Green and the Weel. A reservoir here would do irreparable damage to the cause of conservation by a flooding of an area of importance to research and by control of the flow of the river.

Surely the beautiful Tees, of all northern rivers, was born to run free?

DIAGRAM (not to scale) OF THE UPPER REACHES OF THE TEES AND THE NATURE RESERVES

xxxxx : Nature Reserve boundary
----- : Route of Pennine Way

BRACKEN RIGG TO SAUR HILL

Landranger Sheet 91

Those who walk in Upper Teesdale will increase their enjoyment and understanding of the district if they take with them for information and instruction a publication of the Northumberland and Durham Naturalists' Trust under the title of THE NATURAL HISTORY OF UPPER TEESDALE (obtainable from the Hancock Museum, Newcastle-upon-Tyne, for 5/-, or 5/6 by post).

Saur Hill Bridge has a gate across its middle and good dolerite formations beneath. The route goes up to the farm and thence crosses pastures (stiles, but little evidence of a path) towards an obvious opening in the hills where the Tees is rejoined

"Better a bed down here than a grave up there"....

At Saur Hill Bridge consider the hour and the weather. From here, Dufton is half-a-day's march distant across wild and inhospitable moors, and rain and mist and darkness are enemies to be feared. Nearby is the splendid Youth Hostel, hotel and cottages at Langdon Beck.

Langdon Beck is a river in its own right, with a wide and stony bed that tells of its power in flood.

This detour away from the Tees is untidy, but unavoidable in the absence of a bridge higher up the river.

"Better a living gentian in the field than a dying one in the hand"....

At a certain location on this section of the route (but not indicated here) a little community of the loveliest of Teesdale's floral rarities, the spring gentian, may be noticed. So highly is this plant esteemed that a team of vigilantes ("the Gentian Patrol") keeps a watch on all its known habitats in the flowering season.

Spring Gentian (Gentiana verna)

Over the little rise of Bracken Rigg aim for the corner of the wall and, using a tall stile further along, descend among the rocky outcrops of High Crag to Cronkley and so go forward to, and cross, the bridge. Turn up-river, leaving the Tees in favour of Langdon Beck, as far as Saur Hill Bridge.

A less interesting interlude

High Force

HIGH FORCE TO BRACKEN RIGG

Landranger Sheet 91

High Force is not the highest waterfall in the country, but it is the biggest. No other creates such a profound impression on the senses, no other has such a dramatic yet beautiful setting. The thunderous crash of its waters can be heard from afar : they fall without grace, in a furious rage. It is a spectacle all should see. A great many do, for this is a showplace. A convenient hotel and car park, by the side of the Alston road, and a good path (entered upon payment of a toll) down through the woods ensure a crowded patronage on the Durham side of the river.

High Force occurs where the Tees, after a long restless journey through wild moorlands from its source on Cross Fell, suddenly plunges over a seventy-foot drop in its rocky bed into a wooded gorge buttressed by huge vertical walls. It is a transition in seconds from one extreme to another. Normally there is one fall only ; after heavy rain it is usual for a supplementary fall to appear on the right ; in times of rare spate the full width of the gorge can become a tumult of thrashing water. The scene is enhanced by the dolerite formations and by deep pools overhung by rich foliage.
This is the Tees' finest moment.

The Pennine Way reaches the Force on the Yorkshire (south) side, high above the river, across an open heath of juniper, and the scene is revealed suddenly and not less impressively to the few who use this approach than to the many who walk in procession along the toll path. There is nothing to pay on the Yorkshire side. All is free, wonderful and enjoyable.

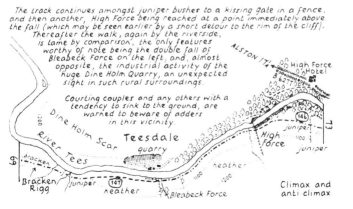

The track continues amongst juniper bushes to a kissing gate in a fence, and then another, High Force being reached at a point immediately above the fall (which may be seen earlier by a short detour to the rim of the cliff).
Thereafter the walk, again by the riverside, is tame by comparison, the only features worthy of note being the double fall of Bleabeck Force on the left, and, almost opposite, the industrial activity of the huge Dine Holm Quarry, an unexpected sight in such rural surroundings.

Courting couples and any others with a tendency to sink to the ground, are warned to beware of adders in this vicinity.

ALSTON 17¼

High Force Hotel

B6277

146

juniper

High Force

juniper

Dine Holm Scar

Teesdale quarry

River Tees

heather

bracken

Bracken Rigg

juniper

147

heather

Bleabeck Force

Climax and anti-climax

Low Force

Although lacking in spectacular features of the quality of High Force and Cauldron Snout, the mile of the Tees between Scoberry Bridge and Low Force is the most beautiful of all. The river bed is wide, and broken by rocky platforms and islands carrying a rich profusion of flowers above normal water level, making a lovely picture enhanced by the columnar formations of the dolerite and the dark woodlands of the Durham side of the river.

Holwick Head
Bridge

The River Tees, below Wynch Bridge

Although the walking as far as Holwick Head Bridge is delightfully simple and straightforward, one hazard must be guarded against: the danger of injury caused by stumbling over crawling botanists in the grass. Upriver from Wynch Bridge they are thick on the ground in summer, and, when trodden on, can recoil and re-act unpleasantly.

HIGH FORCE HOTEL

ROAD B6277   MIDDLETON   Teesdale
71   River Tees

gate and PW sign
Holwick Head Bridge

Holwick Head House (farm)

145   900

Hereabouts the Alston road comes alongside the river. Wynch Bridge is very popular as a picnic-place

Low Force

ROAD B6277

Wynch Bridge (footbridge)

old levels   75

Upon arrival at Holwick Head Bridge do not use the stile in the fence to continue the riverside walk but climb half-left up the open field to a gate in a cross-wall, with various signs and notices. Thence the route is clear onwards. The Teesdale Nature Reserve has now been entered.

A pleasant and popular walk

Upper Teesdale

The Pennine Way, for the greater part of its distance is a walkers' route over desolate uplands — a wilderness walk — but from Middleton, uncharacteristically, it is charted along a course through very colourful riverside meadows before returning to high ground in the company of the Tees. And the Tees is an excellent companion : above Middleton it is a beautiful river, in places sliding smoothly in a wide bed, in places falling and cascading in rocky channels, and it has attracted to it a wealth of lovely trees, a host of darting birds and a fragrant wild flower garden along its banks.   On a sunny June day, the five miles to High Force are a joy to the naturalist, the geologist and the botanist; and to the walker who has tramped the bleak moors from Edale they are perfect delight : this is a place to linger, to rest awhile in sylvan sweetness, and dream.   Upper Teesdale, away from the river, has no greater charms than many places already visited, or that will be visited in the days ahead: no, it is the river, the Tees, with its bordering carpet of flowers, that enchants the eye and uplifts the heart .... and yet makes a man sad because, having found this Arcadia, he must leave it and may never return.

The River Tees, near Middleton

A plan must be made at Middleton. The next stage is a long 20 miles to Dufton, crossing the Pennines into Westmorland by way of wild and lonely moors, yet there are highlights of incomparable scenic quality along the route and much else of absorbing interest. The journey may be broken at Langdon Beck, and should be, for not often does one travel in such charming and fascinating surroundings.   Always tarry long in the presence of beauty, for so much in life is barren.

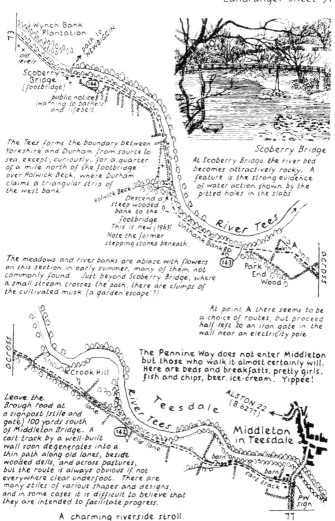

Wynch Bank Plantation

PATH TO NEWBIGGIN

old levels

Scoberry Bridge (footbridge)

144

public notice (warning to bathers and lifebelt

Scoberry Bridge

At Scoberry Bridge the river bed becomes attractively rocky. A feature is the strong evidence of water action shown by the pitted holes in the slabs

The Tees forms the boundary between Yorkshire and Durham from source to sea, except, curiously, for a quarter of a mile north of the footbridge over Holwick Beck, where Durham claims a triangular strip of the west bank

Holwick Beck

Descend a steep wooded bank to the footbridge. This is new (1963) Note the former stepping stones beneath.

Unthank Bank

River Tees

143

Park End Wood

A

across

The meadows and river banks are ablaze with flowers on this section in early summer, many of them not commonly found. Just beyond Scoberry Bridge, where a small stream crosses the path, there are clumps of the cultivated musk (a garden escape?)

At point A there seems to be a choice of routes, but proceed half-left to an iron gate in the wall near an electricity pole.

across

Crook Hill

River Teesdale

ALSTON 22 (B 6277)

The Pennine Way does not enter Middleton but those who walk it almost certainly will. Here are beds and breakfasts, pretty girls, fish and chips, beer, ice-cream. Yippee!

142

old lane

old lane

Middleton in Teesdale

Leave the Brough road at a signpost (stile and gate) 100 yards south of Middleton Bridge. A cart track by a well-built wall soon degenerates into a thin path along old lanes, beside wooded dells, and across pastures, but the route is always obvious if not everywhere clear underfoot. There are many stiles of various shapes and designs, and in some cases it is difficult to believe that they are intended to facilitate progress.

barn

barn

cart track

PW sign

A charming riverside stroll.

77

YORKSHIRE (N.R)

Kirkcarrion is a familiar landmark on the Teesdale section of the walk, its dark cap of trees identifying it unmistakably.
First seen from Tan Hill, it re-appears in the view at odd intervals as successive ridges are surmounted, only finally passing from the scene as the vicinity of Langdon Beck, several miles north, is reached.

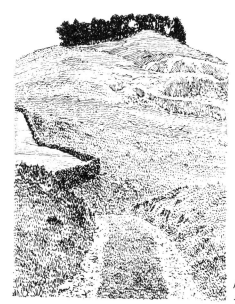

Kirkcarrion, from the B.6276 road.

Look inside this ruin west of Kirkcarrion. A few remaining upright slabs of stone divide the interior into stalls or compartments, suggesting that the building was a stable, possibly for ponies used in the nearby quarry (now closed).

Grassholme Bridge

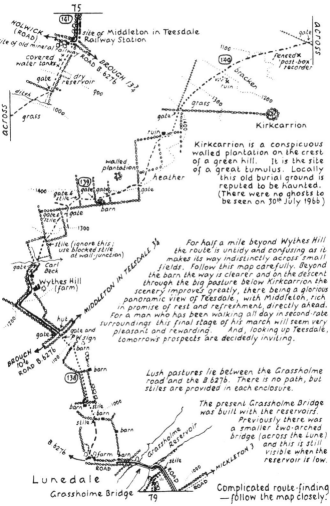

Kirkcarrion is a conspicuous walled plantation on the crest of a green hill. It is the site of a great tumulus. Locally this old burial ground is reputed to be haunted. (There were no ghosts to be seen on 30th July 1966.)

For half a mile beyond Wythes Hill the route is untidy and confusing as it makes its way indistinctly across small fields. Follow this map carefully. Beyond the barn the way is clearer and on the descent through the big pasture below Kirkcarrion the scenery improves greatly, there being a glorious panoramic view of Teesdale, with Middleton, rich in promise of rest and refreshment, directly ahead. For a man who has been walking all day in second-rate surroundings this final stage of his march will seem very pleasant and rewarding. And, looking up Teesdale, tomorrow's prospects are decidedly inviting.

Lush pastures lie between the Grassholme road and the B 6276. There is no path, but stiles are provided in each enclosure.

The present Grassholme Bridge was built with the reservoirs. Previously there was a smaller two-arched bridge (across the Lune) and this is still visible when the reservoir is low.

Complicated route-finding — follow the map closely!

Map amended 1994.

High Birk Hat

There is a dearth of good subjects for the camera hereabouts, but the neat group of buildings at High Birk Hat, just off the route, well merits an inch or two of film.

Above Blackton Bridge the construction of the Balderhead Reservoir, and its ancillary works, have transformed the landscape. The River Balder, once free, and running a course of its own choice, is captive now, its flow controlled both in direction and quantity.
   No banks of flowers now.....
   Concrete runways!
   No more exhilarating days of joyous spate and leaping waters....
   So many measured gallons per minute — no more, no less!
   Life has gone from it.
   A river has died.
   Been killed.
   By the hand of man.

BALDERSDALE TO LUNEDALE

Landranger Sheet 92

This is the crossing from Baldersdale to Lunedale, an easy passage with little climbing. On the descent to Beck Head the new Selset Reservoir is in view on the left, looking very much like Balderhead Reservoir. In fact, because of water-impounding works, Lunedale is almost a repeat of Baldersdale.

Both Hazelgarth Rigg and Kelton Bottom are tracts of uncultivated moor, unkempt deserts of rushes and rough grass, in complete contrast to the rich pastures and tidy husbandry of the Baldersdale and Lunedale farmlands.

There are two tracks over Hazelgarth Rigg, the official one being to the left, the better one to the right. On the top of the Rigg there is a view forwards across Lunedale to Kirkcarrion's clump of trees, overlooking Teesdale.

Baldersdale has been taken over for water supply in a big way. Upstream of Blackton Bridge is the tremendous dam of the new Balderhead Reservoir — the largest earth dam in the country, 3030' long, 157' high, holding back four million gallons of water — with the River Balder emerging from a tunnel.

From Blackton Bridge an old cart-track climbs a pleasant grassy bank to the second of two iron gates in the Water Board wall, from which a small paddock is crossed to a wooden gate near an ash tree, behind Birk Hat.

Not bad, not bad.

The right of way through the field east of How farm is disputed: this route has the best view of Grassholme Bridge. The alternative is to continue along the road, turning down left at the crossroads.

Strange towers away on the right indicate the line of a two-mile water tunnel linking reservoirs in Lunedale and Baldersdale.

— this is a difficult stile topped by barbed wire. To avoid an impasse up aloft, start the climb with the right foot first, not the left.

BALDERSDALE IS THE MID-POINT OF THE PENNINE WAY

According to the sign at the gate on the roadside (but not the O.S.) Hat should be spelled Hatt.

BALDER HEAD — an unkind reminder to wayfarers who are losing their hair.

How (farm)

gates

gate

131

1000

Beck Head (barn) — two gates

gate × two gateposts

× bield

Kelton Bottom

grass and rushes

1100

stile

stile

Mickleton Moor

136

Hazelgarth Rigg

1200

1200

gate and P.W. sign

ROAD — ROMALDKIRK 4½

gate and P.W. sign

1100

High Birk Hat (farm)

gateways — barn

Baldersdale

1000

135 gate

Blackton Bridge

Birk Hat (farm)

R. Balder

Blackton Reservoir

81

BALDERSDALE

ROAD

77

North of Stainmore

Between the busy Stainmore road with its speeding traffic and the quiet Brough-Middleton road lies a sprawling moorland that has always escaped the headlines, is little known generally, and is rarely visited by the fraternity of walkers. It has no peaks, no natural wonders. It is a rolling waste of heather and rushes and rough grass declining to the east from the lonely Westmorland boundary, and intersected by three upland valleys also draining eastwards the watercourses of Deepdale Beck, the River Balder and the River Lune, the gathering grounds of which, over an area of 20 square miles, are without human habitations. Little has changed here since the glaciers receded, but its potentialities as a source of water supply have resulted in the transformation of the Balder and Lune valleys, each of which now holds a string of reservoirs where once cattle and sheep grazed. Baldersdale and Lunedale are side-valleys of Teesdale, and their main appeal is concerned less with the landscape than with the sense of peace prevailing over the scene.

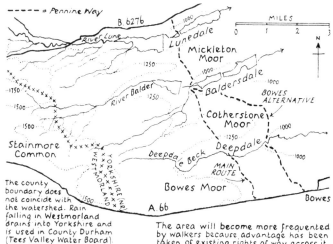

= Pennine Way

B.6276

River Lune

MILES
0   1   2   3

N

Lunedale

Mickleton Moor

1000

1250

1000

Baldersdale

1000

BOWES ALTERNATIVE

1750

River Balder

1250

Cotherstone Moor

1500

1000

1500

1250

Deepdale

Stainmore Common

YORKSHIRE (N.R.)
WESTMORLAND

Deepdale Beck

1000

MAIN ROUTE

The county boundary does not coincide with the watershed. Rain falling in Westmorland drains into Yorkshire and is used in County Durham (Tees Valley Water Board)

1500

Bowes Moor

A.66

Bowes

Footbridge over Deepdale Beck

The area will become more frequented by walkers because advantage has been taken of existing rights of way across it, hitherto little used, in determining the route of the Pennine Way. The wildest part, extending west to the wastelands of Stainmore Common, is avoided, and a milder course followed: in fine weather a simple walk. But this will never be an appealing section: the surroundings are uninteresting, the contours uninspiring, the distant views too distant to impress. Only in August, when Bowes Moor is a purple blaze, is there colour in the scene.

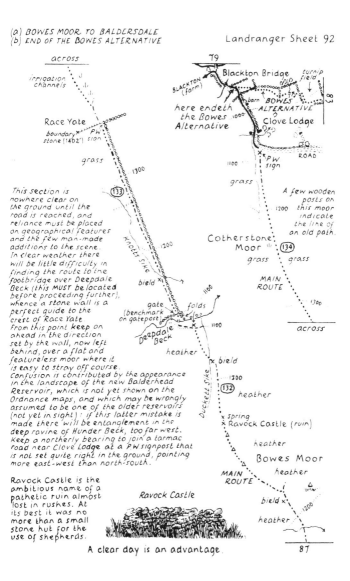

(a) BOWES MOOR TO BALDERSDALE
(b) END OF THE BOWES ALTERNATIVE

Landranger Sheet 92

across

irrigation channels

Race Yate
boundary stone (1402')
PW sign

grass

1300

Blackton Bridge
BLACKTON (farm)
turnip field
here endeth the Bowes Alternative
barn
BOWES ALTERNATIVE
Clove Lodge
ROAD
PW sign
grass

A few wooden posts on this moor indicate the line of an old path.

Cotherstone Moor
grass   grass
MAIN ROUTE
1300
across

This section is nowhere clear on the ground until the road is reached, and reliance must be placed on geographical features and the few man-made additions to the scene. In clear weather there will be little difficulty in finding the route to the footbridge over Deepdale Beck (this MUST be located before proceeding further), whence a stone wall is a perfect guide to the crest of Race Yate. From this point keep on ahead in the direction set by the wall, now left behind, over a flat and featureless moor where it is easy to stray off course. Confusion is contributed by the appearance in the landscape of the new Balderhead Reservoir, which is not yet shown on the Ordnance maps, and which may be wrongly assumed to be one of the older reservoirs (not yet in sight): if this latter mistake is made there will be entanglement in the deep ravine of Hunder Beck, too far west. Keep a northerly bearing to join a tarmac road near Clove Lodge at a PW signpost that is not set quite right in the ground, pointing more east-west than north-south.

Knotts Sike
1200
bield
gate (benchmark on gatepost)
folds
Deepdale Beck
heather
bield
Duckett Sike
1200
132 heather
spring
Ravock Castle (ruin)
heather
Bowes Moor
heather
MAIN ROUTE
bield
heather
1200

Ravock Castle is the ambitious name of a pathetic ruin almost lost in rushes. At its best it was no more than a small stone hut for the use of shepherds.

Ravock Castle

A clear day is an advantage.

87

82

Goldsborough

Goldsborough is a flat-topped mound with a cap of millstone that has survived the ages, and rises prominently above the surrounding moorland. Overhangs in the rocks provide excellent shelter.

The escarpment

The millstone cap

The ruins of Levy Pool

STONY KELD TO BALDERSDALE

Baldersdale

There is no obvious path in the eight fields from East Friar House to the Blackton road but stiles and gates are provided.

East Friar House (farm)

barn

West Friar House (farm)

COTHERSTONE S

cattle grid

1100

ROAD

CLOVE LODGE ¾

Goldsborough
1274

1200

1200

irrigation channels

across

Yawd Sike

across

Yawd Sike

rushes

grass

West Loups's (in ruins)

ruin

ARMY TRAINING AREA
DANGER
KEEP OUT

1200

grass

Hare Sike

1200

To the north of Deepdale Beck there is a mile of unattractive and featureless territory. Four minor ridges and three little becks are crossed in an unexciting series of undulations. When the military fence is joined a fair track materialises: this is followed to a cross-wall near a ruin, where a better prospect opens up. Ahead is Goldsborough, which, alone amongst these rolling uplands, has a distinctive outline and some welcome rocks.

Note the graveyard of trees north-east of Deepdale Beck.

The ford across the beck at Levy Pool is unfordable by travellers on foot, but there is an easier passage 50 yards upstream.

Blackpool Sike

grass

1200

bracken

grass

Hazelgill Beck

bracken

1100

grass

Deepdale Beck

Levy Pool (in ruins) (or Laverpool)

barn

cart track

ruin

gates

Stony Keld (farm)

This depressing announcement appears on red notice-boards at frequent intervals alongside the route and around the perimeter of a large area to the east. The place is a shambles : the military have taken over. Walls are broken, buildings are ghostly ruins, good earth lies unkempt, natural beauty is withered and dead. Those who lived here, man and beast, have found pastures new.

The killers are in.

Levy Pool is, presumably, a victim of economics, not of the military. It is a sad thing to see the gaunt skeleton of what was once a farmhouse of much character with thatched outbuildings. Backed by trees, the house faces south — but its sightless eyes will never see the sun again.

Uninspiring!

Map slightly revised 1994 to show amended route to Stony Keld.

THE LAWS OF EXCLUSION

*Extracts from a letter by Harry Appleyard,
published in Cumbria, June 1966*

"For some months I have been engaged in a survey of the Northern Pennines.....

"Travelling northwards from Stainmore one encounters gathering grounds of the Tees Valley Water Board, infantry training ranges near Barnard Castle, grouse moors around Middleton in Teesdale, the Upper Teesdale Nature Reserve from about High Force onwards, the Army firing range on Mickle Fell, and then the Moor House Nature Reserve lying between the Eden Valley and the Tees — roughly a hundred square miles of country in which the humble walker is not particularly welcome. In fact, at Cauldron Snout, probably the finest mountain cascade in England, the firing range and the two Nature Reserves practically join up, and the Water Board are proposing to move in with a new reservoir.

"Incidentally, I don't think one is particularly safe on the rights-of-way, either; there is more than one bull roaming loose in the vast upland pastures of Teesdale possessed of the same fine disregard for the individual's puny rights.

"It should not be concluded from the above that I am 'agin' these various bodies, or for that matter their local representatives, who are usually courteous and helpful. .... What I am against is the allocation of large tracts of land by Governments to various departments *with built-in power to make their own laws of exclusion.*

"We must have water supplies, defence projects, forestry and agriculture and scientific studies, but these things can exist without exclusion of recreational facilities....."

Desolation and Devastation

A scene of desolation can be very beautiful; a scene of devastation is always downright ugly. Nature fashions desolation; man causes devastation. Nature's wildernesses often have charm; man's wildernesses are without charm. The desolate Sleightholme Moor impresses; the derelict Air Ministry site depresses. Nature creates; man destroys.

...like croquet hoops against the sky

*Evening silhouette,
Air Ministry property, Tute Hill*

THE GRETA VALLEY TO TUTE HILL   Landranger Sheet 92

Bowes Castle

— a Norman watch-tower commanding a view of the approaches from Stainmore, probably built as a garrison outpost. It stands on a part of the site of a Roman Fort, the ramparts of which can still be traced in the field above the River Greta.
(Ministry of Works. Admission free.!)

There is an alternative route at Tute Hill; keep north along the road passing Stony Keld and Strand Foot; stay with the road until West Stony Keld where the main route is rejoined.

If the river is in spate, continue on the track after Lady Mires farm until Gilmonby is reached, and cross the bridge there.

Map revised 1994.

After Lady Mires farm, turn left off the track and go down to the river bank. Using stepping stones near the weir, cross the river and climb the path to Swinholme. A tarmacked track then swings north, but half way along, turn right over a fence and head east across the hollow of a field to a gate, then cross more fields via stiles to cut across the remains of the Roman fort of Lavatrae. A narrow side road leads into the main street of Bowes.

God's Bridge

There are several natural rock bridges over streams in the limestone districts of the northern counties, formed by the erosive action of water, and God's Bridge is a happy choice of name for many of them. God's Bridge on the Greta, near Pasture End, is a splendid example: here is an intrusion of limestone in the native millstone grit of Stainmore and the river characteristically pursues an underground course, the stony bed being dry except in times of flood, but beneath the bridge a dark deep pool is fed by seepage through crevices in the rock walls, and is a permanent feature of this interesting scene.

For centuries the bridge has been in use for the passage of men and their animals — an ancient drove way crosses it.

(a) SLEIGHTHOLME TO PASTURE END
(b) SLEIGHTHOLME TO THE GRETA VALLEY   Landranger Sheet 92

The Bowes Alternative ("the Bowes Loop") makes a wide detour to the east of several miles, and its description will occupy a few pages exclusively. The Main Route is resumed on page 81, where the Bowes Loop will be seen joining in at the end of its wanderings.

81

131
gate   Pasture
       End   BOWES 2¼
BROUGH 10 ROAD
       gate   A.66   1100
and P.W.sign
Rock Bridge   line of former railway
cottages   River Greta
God's
Bridge   River Greta   1000
                                              East
                                              Mellwaters
                                              (farm)
       West   Sleightholme Beck
       Mellwaters
       (farm)   gate   An instructive companion
MAIN   for this district is a booklet,
ROUTE   gate   "From Stainmore to the Tees",
       1100   by D.M.Ramsden, M.Sc., M.Ed.
                           1100   (Dalesman Publishing Co)
       BOWES
       ALTERNATIVE   At the busy A.66 at Pasture End
wall   there is a sudden and startling
to be   heather   return to modern civilisation
climbed   after the quietness of the hills,
(barbed wire)   130   and danger from fast traffic in
A stile is needed.   crossing the few yards of tarmac.
                                        Once through the opposite gate
Wytham Moor   peace as suddenly returns. It
                                        is a momentary nightmare.
Pasture End comes into view   Trough
                              Heads
       1200   (farm)   At Trough Heads, a
                                        fateful decision must be
       heather   gate   made — whether it is better
                                        to push on over the moors in the
                                        hope of reaching accommodation
                                        before nightfall, and in the event
                                        of failure to do so, possibly perish
                              Q   in the satisfying knowledge that the
                        Intake   end came honourably on the main Way
       gate   Bridge   and not on a soft alternative; or to
                                        go down with the Greta through lush
Bog Scar   gate   BOWES   pastures to sample the allurements of
                    (ROAD)   Bowes. If the day is far advanced, as it
       1200   barn   probably will be, the short answer is Bowes,
The   gate &   and to hell with glory and gold medals. You
Bog   P.W.sign   barn   once knew a girl who lived at Bowes. You are
                    129   dying for a drink. Down to Bowes, lads!
                    Jack Shields
                    Bridge
                    gates   Of the two choices of route available between
       89   Sleightholme   Sleightholme and Trough Heads, the better
                                        is that crossing the beck at Intake Bridge.

West
Charity
Pasture
(farm)
85

A.66

River Greta
gates

Easy walking, increasing in interest.

Sleightholme

A cairn on Sleightholme Moor

Tan Hill Inn

The glories of Tan Hill Inn belong to the past. For centuries it was a focal point of much commercial and industrial activity, an important meeting-place of trade routes. It was a packhorse halt and a refuge for travellers. Coal from the nearby mines passed by in transit for the surrounding dales.

All this is changed. Now the inn is quiet, left with its one remaining distinction as the highest in England.

Tan Hill Inn

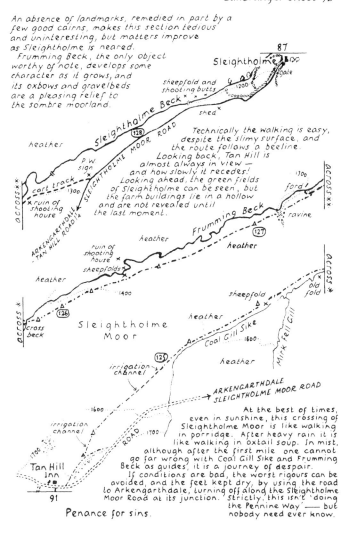

TAN HILL TO SLEIGHTHOLME

Landranger Sheet 92

An absence of landmarks, remedied in part by a few good cairns, makes this section tedious and uninteresting, but matters improve as Sleightholme is neared.
Frumming Beck, the only object worthy of note, develops some character as it grows, and its oxbows and gravelbeds are a pleasing relief to the sombre moorland.

Sleightholme

sheepfold and shooting butts

shed

Sleightholme Beck

heather

P.W. sign

cart track

ruin of shooting house

Technically the walking is easy, despite the slimy surface, and the route follows a beeline.
Looking back, Tan Hill is almost always in view — and how slowly it recedes!
Looking ahead, the green fields of Sleightholme can be seen, but the farm buildings lie in a hollow and are not revealed until the last moment.

ford

ravine

Frumming Beck

heather

heather

ruin of shooting house

sheepfolds

heather

old fold

sheepfold

Sleightholme Moor

heather

Coal Gill Sike

heather

Mirk Fell Gill

cross beck

irrigation channel

ARKENGARTHDALE SLEIGHTHOLME MOOR ROAD

irrigation channel

ROAD

Tan Hill Inn

At the best of times, even in sunshine, this crossing of Sleightholme Moor is like walking in porridge. After heavy rain it is like walking in oxtail soup. In mist, although after the first mile one cannot go far wrong with Coal Gill Sike and Frumming Beck as guides, it is a journey of despair.
If conditions are bad, the worst rigours can be avoided, and the feet kept dry, by using the road to Arkengarthdale, turning off along the Sleightholme Moor Road at its junction. Strictly, this isn't 'doing the Pennine Way' —— but nobody need ever know.

Penance for sins.

YORKSHIRE (N.R.)

The approach to Tan Hill Inn from the south

Derelict air shafts, Tanhill Colliery

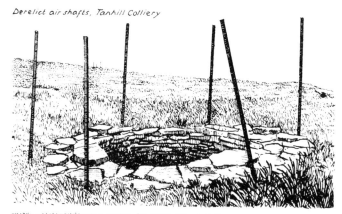

The moors around Tan Hill are pitted with derelict and abandoned shafts, dangerous relics of the old collieries.

Those persons or bodies responsible for safety fencing are likely to have a tragedy on their conscience one of these days.

Don't walk in the dark on Tan Hill!

The two shafts illustrated are within 150 yards of the P.W. route

KELD TO TAN HILL

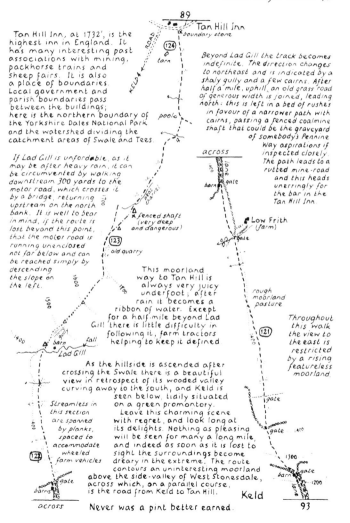

89

Tan Hill Inn
boundary stone

Tan Hill Inn, at 1732', is the highest inn in England. It has many interesting past associations with mining, packhorse trains and sheep fairs. It is also a place of boundaries. Local government and parish boundaries pass between the buildings; here is the northern boundary of the Yorkshire Dales National Park and the watershed dividing the catchment areas of Swale and Tees.

Beyond Lad Gill the track becomes indefinite. The direction changes to northeast and is indicated by a shaly gully and a few cairns. After half a mile, uphill, an old grass road of generous width is joined, leading north: this is left in a bed of rushes in favour of a narrower path with cairns, passing a fenced coalmine shaft that could be the graveyard of somebody's Pennine Way aspirations if inspected closely. The path leads to a rutted mine-road and this heads unerringly for the bar in the Tan Hill Inn.

If Lad Gill is unfordable, as it may be after heavy rain, it can be circumvented by walking downstream 300 yards to the motor road, which crosses it by a bridge, returning upstream on the north bank. It is well to bear in mind, if the route is lost beyond this point, that the motor road is running unenclosed not far below and can be reached simply by descending the slope on the left.

A fenced shaft (very deep and dangerous)

old quarry

This moorland way to Tan Hill is always very juicy underfoot; after rain it becomes a ribbon of water. Except for a half-mile beyond Lad Gill there is little difficulty in following it, farm tractors helping to keep it defined

Low Frith (farm)

rough moorland pasture

Throughout this walk the view to the east is restricted by a rising featureless moorland

As the hillside is ascended after crossing the Swale there is a beautiful view in retrospect of its wooded valley curving away to the south, and Keld is seen below, tidily situated on a green promontory.
    Leave this charming scene with regret, and look long at its delights. Nothing as pleasing will be seen for many a long mile, and indeed as soon as it is lost to sight the surroundings become dreary in the extreme. The route contours an uninteresting moorland above the side-valley of West Stonesdale, across which, on a parallel course, is the road from Keld to Tan Hill.

Streamlets in this section are spanned by planks, spaced to accommodate wheeled farm vehicles

across

Keld

Never was a pint better earned.

93

Keld

Kisdon Force

Kisdon

THWAITE TO KELD

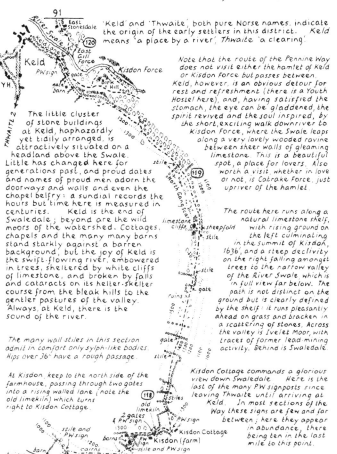

'Keld' and 'Thwaite', both pure Norse names, indicate the origin of the early settlers in this district. Keld means 'a place by a river', Thwaite 'a clearing'.

Note that the route of the Pennine Way does not visit either the hamlet of Keld or Kisdon Force but passes between. Keld, however, is an obvious detour for rest and refreshment (there is a Youth Hostel here), and, having satisfied the stomach, the eye can be gladdened, the spirit revived and the soul inspired, by the short, exciting walk downriver to Kisdon Force, where the Swale leaps along a very lovely wooded ravine between sheer walls of gleaming limestone. This is a beautiful spot, a place for lovers. Also worth a visit, whether in love or not, is Catrake Force, just upriver of the hamlet.

The little cluster of stone buildings at Keld, haphazardly yet tidily arranged, is attractively situated on a headland above the Swale. Little has changed here for generations past, and proud dates and names of proud men adorn the doorways and walls and even the chapel belfry: a sundial records the hours but time here is measured in centuries. Keld is the end of Swaledale; beyond are the wild moors of the watershed. Cottages, chapels and the many many barns stand starkly against a barren background, but the joy of Keld is the swift-flowing river, embowered in trees, sheltered by white cliffs of limestone, and broken by falls and cataracts on its helter-skelter course from the bleak hills to the gentler pastures of the valley. Always, at Keld, there is the sound of the river.

The route here runs along a natural limestone shelf, with rising ground on the left culminating in the summit of Kisdon, 1636, and a steep declivity on the right falling amongst trees to the narrow valley of the River Swale which is in full view far below. The path is not distinct on the ground but is clearly defined by the shelf: it runs pleasantly ahead on grass and bracken in a scattering of stones. Across the valley is Ivelet Moor, with traces of former lead mining activity. Behind is Swaledale.

The many wall stiles in this section admit in comfort only sylph-like bodies. Hips over 36" have a rough passage.

At Kisdon, keep to the north side of the farmhouse, passing through two gates into a rising walled lane (note the old limekiln) which turns right to Kisdon Cottage.

Kisdon Cottage commands a glorious view down Swaledale. Here is the last of the many PW signposts since leaving Thwaite until arriving at Keld. In most sections of the Way these signs are few and far between; here they appear in abundance, there being ten in the last mile to this point.

The exit from Thwaite eastwards is complicated by small walled enclosures and off-route footpaths. After passing through 2 stiles (PW sign at the second) strike north-east across the next field, using a gate with a barn on the right. Ignore the clearer riverside path

A magnificent terrace high above the Swale

Cottages at Thwaite
(TV aerials
omitted)

above:
Ruin and spoil heaps,
Trial Level near Thwaite

left:
Beacon, north-east shoulder
of Great Shunner Fell

GREAT SHUNNER FELL TO THWAITE

Landranger Sheet 98

Swaledale has a very long history of lead mining going back to Roman times, especially near the middle reaches of the valley, but falling yield and foreign competition resulted in the final closure of the mines last century. It is likely that the old trial level met on the descent (now sealed) was driven in connection with a nearby lead mine although the black spoil gives the impression that coal was extracted.

Q: Which is the most beautiful of the Yorkshire Dales?
A: Swaledale.
Q: Next?
A: Wharfedale.

A: MUKER 1, RICHMOND 21
B: HAWES 6

NOTE: There are no public conveniences at Thwaite so you had better do it in this lane.

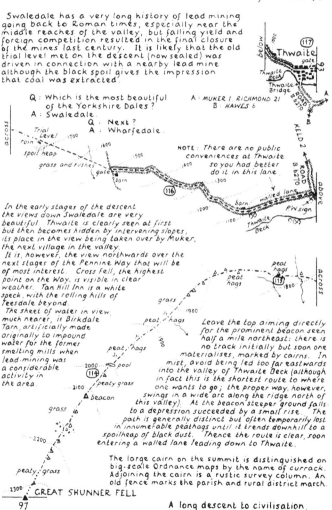

In the early stages of the descent the views down Swaledale are very beautiful. Thwaite is clearly seen at first but then becomes hidden by intervening slopes, its place in the view being taken over by Muker, the next village in the valley.
It is, however, the view northwards over the next stages of the Pennine Way that will be of most interest. Cross Fell, the highest point on the Way, is visible in clear weather. Tan Hill Inn is a white speck, with the rolling hills of Teesdale beyond.
The sheet of water in view, much nearer, is Birkdale Tarn, artificially made originally to impound water for the former smelting mills when lead-mining was a considerable activity in the area.

Leave the top aiming directly for the prominent beacon seen half a mile northeast: there is no track initially but soon one materialises, marked by cairns. In mist, avoid being led too far eastwards into the valley of Thwaite Beck (although in fact this is the shortest route to where one wants to go; the proper way, however, swings in a wide arc along the ridge north of this valley). At the beacon steeper ground falls to a depression succeeded by a small rise. The path is generally distinct but often temporarily lost in innumerable peathags until it trends downhill to a spoilheap of black dust. Thence the route is clear, soon entering a walled lane leading down to Thwaite.

The large cairn on the summit is distinguished on big-scale Ordnance maps by the name of currack. Adjoining the cairn is a rustic survey column. An old fence marks the parish and rural district march.

GREAT SHUNNER FELL

A long descent to civilisation.

Great Shunner Fell

*Summit cairn
and Ordnance column*

Great Shunner Fell is the highest ground yet reached on the Pennine Way, coming from the south. It is also the highest central ground on the 54° 22' latitude between the west coast and the east coast. But it is not situated on the main watershed. Its streams all ultimately find their way into the North Sea, eastwards. It is a minor watershed only, a lateral one between Swale and Ure, yet does not, in fact, give birth to either. The true watershed in the vicinity is a few miles west, on Abbotside Common, which divides Eden and Ure.

Robbed of this distinction, Great Shunner Fell has nevertheless many features of interest. It certainly is *great*. It is of massive girth, covering some twenty square miles, and although its lower slopes provide easy and pleasant walking much of the sprawling top is desolated by peat hags and extensive areas of wet moss. These do not deter the walker who is merely traversing the fell and not exploring its wildernesses for a fairly good cairned track, which is destined to improve under the tread of more and more boots, is a safe conductor throughout the long walk, faltering only on the crossing of the summit, a deficiency of no consequence in clear visibility.

It is as a viewpoint that Great Shunner Fell excels, the panorama being widespread in all directions. There is a charming view of Swaledale, better seen on the descent to Thwaite, but mainly the prospect is of wild rolling moors stretching far into the distance, relieved by the sharper outlines of the magnificent twins of Ribblesdale, Ingleborough and, of recent memory, Penyghent. The real glory of the view, however, is the western horizon, formed by a serrated range of peaks: the magic mountains of the Lake District, tremendously exciting even from afar.

A further attraction of Great Shunner Fell, for most people, is the remarkable ease of its ascent, the five miles of its south ridge from Hardrow surely ranking as the easiest fellclimb of all.

A notable feature of the fell is its series of beacons, ten in number, soundly constructed. Two are met en route, others seen at a distance.

Crag End Beacon

Landranger Sheet 98

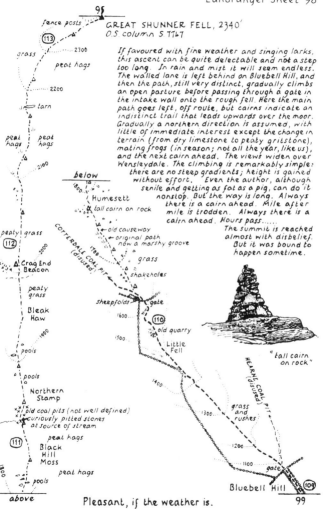

GREAT SHUNNER FELL, 2340'
O.S. column S.7767

If favoured with fine weather and singing larks,
this ascent can be quite delectable and not a step
too long. In rain and mist it will seem endless.
The walled lane is left behind on Bluebell Hill, and
then the path, still very distinct, gradually climbs
an open pasture before passing through a gate in
the intake wall onto the rough fell. Here the main
path goes left, off route, but cairns indicate an
indistinct trail that leads upwards over the moor.
Gradually a northern direction is assumed, with
little of immediate interest except the change in
terrain (from dry limestone to peaty gritstone),
mating frogs (in season; not all the year, like us),
and the next cairn ahead. The views widen over
Wensleydale. The climbing is remarkably simple:
there are no steep gradients; height is gained
without effort. Even the author, although
senile and getting as fat as a pig, can do it
nonstop. But the way is long. Always
there is a cairn ahead. Mile after
mile is trodden. Always there is a
cairn ahead. Hours pass......
The summit is reached
almost with disbelief.
But it was bound to
happen sometime.

95

fence posts

113

grass   2300

peat hags

2200

tarn

peat   peat
hags   hags

2100

peaty grass

112

Crag End
Beacon

peaty
grass

Bleak
Haw

1900

pools

pools

Northern
Stamp

old coal pits (not well defined)
curiously pitted stones
at source of stream

peat hags

111   Black
            Hill
            Moss

peat hags

1800   pools

above

below

1800

Humesett
tall cairn on rock

old causeway
original path
now a marshy groove
grass

shakeholes

sheepfolds   gate

1600   110

            old quarry

1500   Little
            Fell

1400

COTTERDALE COAL PIT
(disused)

1700

2000

1300

HEARNE COAL PIT
(disused)

"tall cairn
on rock"

grass
and
rushes

1200

1100   gate

Bluebell Hill   109

Pleasant, if the weather is.

Hardrow Force

HAWES TO BLUEBELL HILL

Landranger Sheet 98

A quarter-mile off route is England's highest waterfall* in a magnificent setting at the head of a limestone gorge, and those who have not yet seen this fine spectacle, Hardrow Force, should certainly take the opportunity of doing so. Access to it is through the Green Dragon Inn on payment of a small fee, and alongside a graveyard on a much-trodden path. A dilapidated bandstand at the entrance to the gorge, overlooked by crumbling terraces of seats, tells of the heyday of Hardrow, when band contests were annually held in this natural auditorium and attracted large crowds. The Force itself, however, has lost nothing in impressiveness with the passing of time and is revealed around a bend, falling gracefully in a single leap of 96 feet over a lip of limestone. The brave thing to do is to walk beneath the overhang behind the fall: if this is done a return may be made down the right bank to a footbridge.

The older spelling of Hardrow is Hardraw

* The highest *above ground*. There are many higher falls in potholes within 20 miles of Hardrow. e.g. Fell Beck on Ingleborough falls 340 feet into Gaping Gill.

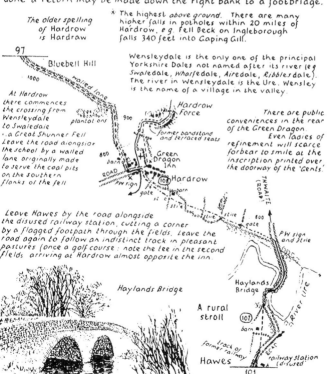

Wensleydale is the only one of the principal Yorkshire Dales not named after its river (e.g. Swaledale, Wharfedale, Airedale, Ribblesdale). The river in Wensleydale is the Ure. Wensley is the name of a village in the valley.

97

Bluebell Hill

1000

walled lane

At Hardrow there commences the crossing from Wensleydale to Swaledale ..a Great Shunner Fell. Leave the road alongside the school by a walled lane originally made to serve the coal pits on the southern flanks of the fell

plantations

900

Hardrow Force

former bandstand and terraced seats

800

barn

Green Dragon Inn

ROAD

There are public conveniences in the rear of the Green Dragon.
Even ladies of refinement will scarce forbear to smile at the inscription printed over the doorway of the 'Gents'.

106

Hardrow

PW sign

gate

barn

stile

THWAITE (ROAD)

Leave Hawes by the road alongside the disused railway station, cutting a corner by a flagged footpath through the fields. Leave the road again to follow an indistinct track in pleasant pastures (once a golf course : note the tee in the second fields) arriving at Hardrow almost opposite the inn.

stile

stile

800

gate

PW sign and stile

Haylands Bridge

Haylands Bridge

A rural stroll

107

barn

track of former railway

Hawes

railway station (disused)

River Ure

101

YORKSHIRE (N.R.)

Hawes, the market town of upper Wensleydale, an urban community with rural interests, is a small and compact 'built-up area' crowded alongside a busy main street, the A.684, (Kendal-Northallerton) and its quaint arrangement of alleyways and cottages can have changed little in the past two centuries. It's declining population (about 1,100) and visitors are well catered for by shops, cafes and inns.

Market day: Tuesday
Early closing: Wednesday

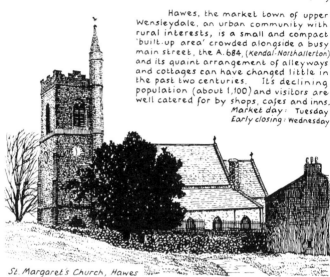

St. Margaret's Church, Hawes

Gayle

WEST CAM ROAD TO HAWES

Landranger Sheet 98

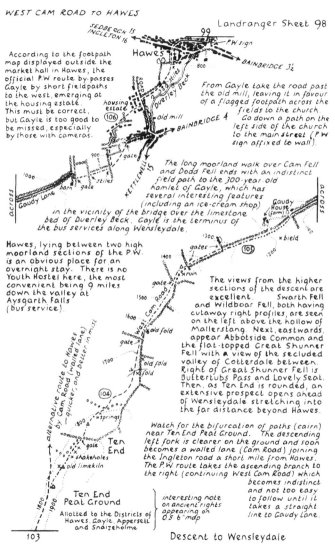

According to the footpath map displayed outside the market hall in Hawes, the official P.W. route by-passes Gayle by short fieldpaths to the west, emerging at the housing estate. This must be correct, but Gayle is too good to be missed, especially by those with cameras.

From Gayle take the road past the old mill, leaving it in favour of a flagged footpath across the fields to the church. Go down a path on the left side of the church to the main street (P W sign affixed to wall).

The long moorland walk over Cam Fell and Dodd Fell ends with an indistinct field path to the 300-year-old hamlet of Gayle, which has several interesting features (including an ice-cream shop) in the vicinity of the bridge over the limestone bed of Duerley Beck. Gayle is the terminus of the bus services along Wensleydale.

Hawes, lying between two high moorland sections of the P.W. is an obvious place for an overnight stay. There is no Youth Hostel here, the most convenient being 9 miles down the valley at Aysgarth Falls (bus service).

The views from the higher sections of the descent are excellent. Swarth Fell and Wildboar Fell, both having cutaway right profiles, are seen on the left above the hollow of Mallerstang. Next, eastwards, appear Abbotside Common and the flat-topped Great Shunner Fell with a view of the secluded valley of Cotterdale between. Right of Great Shunner Fell is Buttertubs Pass and Lovely Seat. Then, as Ten End is rounded, an extensive prospect opens ahead of Wensleydale stretching into the far distance beyond Hawes.

Watch for the bifurcation of paths (cairn) near Ten End Peat Ground. The descending left fork is clearer on the ground and soon becomes a walled lane (Cam Road) joining the Ingleton road a short mile from Hawes. The P.W. route takes the ascending branch to the right (continuing West Cam Road) which becomes indistinct and not too easy to follow until it takes a straight line to Gaudy Lane.

interesting note on ancient rights appearing on O.S. 6" mdp

Ten End Peat Ground
Allotted to the Districts of Hawes, Gayle, Appersett and Snaizeholme

Descent to Wensleydale

Top map slightly amended 1994.

Great Shunner Fell

West Cam Road

Sinkhole, West Cam Road

at Kidhow Gate. 1877'

THE WATERSHED: Three important river systems have their beginnings in the vicinity of Kidhow Gate. The indefinite slope southeast divides the headwaters of the Ribble and the Wharfe: this watershed is clearer on Ordnance maps than by inspection of the ground. Northwest the moor declines to the valley of Snaizeholme Beck, a feeder of the Ure.
At this point of the Pennine Way the gathering grounds of the Ribble are vacated, those of the Wharfe skirted and those of the Ure entered.

THE COUNTY BOUNDARY: The limestone wall at Cold Keld Gate, which continues to and beyond Kidhow Gate, marks the boundary between the North and West Ridings of Yorkshire. At Cold Keld Gate the West Riding is left behind at long last, having been entered as far to the south as Black Hill above Longdendale, since when the Pennine Way has kept wholly within or along its boundaries except for a few miles north of Blackstone Edge where Lancashire was visited.

At Kidhow Gate, therefore, bleak and inhospitable though the place is, there is a sense of accomplishment, of having reached a definite stage of the journey.   Before turning off the road to go north, reflect how this highway over the hills has been used down the centuries — first as a military way by occupying forces, then as a trade route in the days of packhorses, then as a farm road, and now as an official link in the country's first long-distance walk.   And note the view if the day be clear: Penyghent, Ingleborough, Whernside, Wildboar Fell, Buckden Pike and Great Shunner Fell all appearing prominently in a grand circle of uplands.

Ingleborough

Penyghent

Cam Houses

Cairn and signpost Kidhow Gate
(PW sign missing. 7th & 14th Feb. 1967)

Cairn, Cam High Road

CAM END TO WEST CAM ROAD

Landranger Sheet 98

across ‡

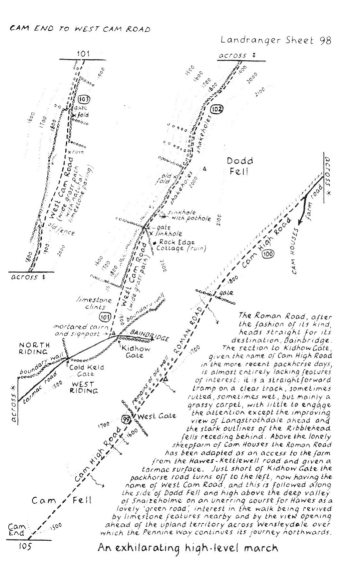

101

103
gate
fold

1800
1700
1600

West Cam Road
(wide grass path
with natural
limestone paving)

x ruin

old fence

1800
1900
2000

across ‡

across ‡

1500
1600
1800
1800
2000
2100

102

shakeholes

Dodd Fell

old path
fold

sinkhole
with pothole
gate
sinkhole
Rock Edge
Cottage (ruin)

West Cam Road
(wide grass path)

1600
1700
1800

2000

across x

farm road

CAM HOUSES

Cam High Road

100

gate

1800

ROMAN ROAD

The Roman Road, after
the fashion of its kind,
heads straight for its
destination, Bainbridge.
The section to Kidhow Gate,
given the name of Cam High Road
in the more recent packhorse days,
is almost entirely lacking features
of interest: it is a straightforward
tramp on a clear track, sometimes
rutted, sometimes wet, but mainly a
grassy carpet, with little to engage
the attention except the improving
view of Langstrothdale ahead and
the stark outlines of the Ribblehead
fells receding behind. Above the lonely
sheepfarm of Cam Houses the Roman Road
has been adapted as an access to the farm
from the Hawes-Kettlewell road and given a
tarmac surface. Just short of Kidhow Gate the
packhorse road turns off to the left, now having the
name of West Cam Road, and this is followed along
the side of Dodd Fell and high above the deep valley
of Snaizeholme on an unerring course for Hawes as a
lovely 'green road', interest in the walk being revived
by limestone features nearby and by the view opening
ahead of the upland territory across Wensleydale over
which the Pennine Way continues its journey northwards.

limestone
clints

West Cam Road
(wide grass path)

101

boundary wall

mortared cairn
and signpost

BAINBRIDGE

NORTH RIDING

boundary wall

Kidhow
Gate

Cold Keld
Gate

WEST RIDING

tarmac road

1500

across x

remains of old wall

99
West Gate

1700
1600

Cam High Road

Cam Fell

Cam End

1500

105

An exhilarating high-level march

YORKSHIRE (W.R.)

Ling Gill Bridge

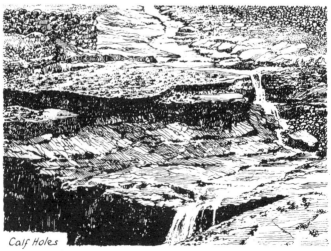

Calf Holes

OLD ING TO CAM END

The desolation of the landscape at Cam End is absolute, yet, going back into history, important military and trade routes have crossed the hills here. The packhorse road from Settle to Hawes, which the Pennine Way 'adopts' at Old Ing, comes up from Horton and, at the cairn, joins and for the next two and a half miles coincides with the Roman Road between Ingleton and the fort at Bainbridge. Where you tread a Roman soldier once trod.

North of Ling Gill Bridge the route enters an expanse of dreary moorland as it starts the long gradual climb to Cam Fell, and although the way continues clear it is badly waterlogged in many places where there is no natural drainage. As height is gained wide views are obtained of Ribblehead and its fells, west, and over Longstrothdale Chase to the east.

North Ribblesdale is notable for its beautiful wooded limestone gills, and the finest of these is Ling Gill, a gorge of striking proportions where the stream cascades in a chaos of boulders nearly 200 feet below the top of vertical walls of rock. The path runs along the rim of the ravine and has good views down into it.

Calf Holes is the last of the named Craven potholes met on the journey and has become a popular weekend picnic spot now that motorists have discovered that they can get their cars as far as Old Ing by road from Horton. Look over the wall; it could be passed unnoticed. A stream is engulfed here and after a long subterranean passage emerges in Browgill Cave. This cave is off-route, but if 20 minutes can be spared it should be visited: it is the finest cave of debouchure within easy reach of the Pennine Way, its attractions including an old lime-kiln in an excellent state of preservation and a miniature gorge. The cave itself can be entered and followed for 70 yards by non-experts. To reach it, turn down the field through a gate at the barn; no footpath.

Charming scenery — at first.

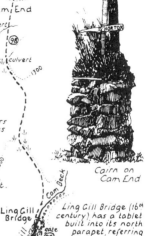

GEARSTONES (ROMAN ROAD) ¼

Cam End

culvert

culvert

Cam Beck

Cairn on Cam End

Ling Gill Bridge

Ling Gill

Ling Gill Bridge (16th century) has a tablet built into its north parapet, referring to its repair in 1765 at 'the charge of the whole West Riding'. Built of gritstone from the bed of Cam Beck, it marks the transition from limestone to peat moorland.

x cave

x pothole

At Old Ing the Settle-Hawes packhorse road is joined. Opposite the farm, turn north along a walled lane in a lather of mud. Beyond the gate a grass path develops, and continues pleasantly to Ling Gill Bridge in scenes of increasing beauty.

barn
kiln

Browgill Cave

Dry Laithe Cave (better known as Calf Holes)

gate   gate

Old Ing

107

Penyghent Long Churn

Jackdaw Hole

Sell Gill Holes

Upper (stream) entrance

Lower (dry) entrance

SELL GILL TO OLD ING

Landranger Sheet 98

Care must be taken to turn off
the packhorse road at the right
place to go across country to
Old Ing, otherwise one may
get badly off course. Where
a wall crosses at a tangent,
immediately after passing
through the gate aim left over
a small hill with a cairn, when the trees of Old Ing
come into sight. This is really a shift from one
packhorse road (Settle - Langstrothdale)
to another (Settle - Hawes).

A feature of the Yorkshire Dales country is
the network of 'green' roads (i.e. grass-covered)
crossing the hills and linking the valleys : relics
of the days when trade was carried on by the use
of horse transport. Where these routes ran along
the valleys they have long been superseded by
tarmac roads, but motors have not been able
to follow the horses over the hills and the high
moorland ways have fallen into disuse ; they
are, however, still plain to see and a joy to
walk upon, being well-graded and sufficiently
distinct on the ground to remove doubts of
route-finding. Often they are walled on one
or both sides ; sometimes they run free and
unfettered across the breasts of the hills and
over the skyline. For pedestrian exercise these
old packhorse roads are excellent : quiet and
traffic-free they lead effortlessly into and
over the hills amid wild and lonely scenery,
green ribbons threading their way through
bog and heather and rushes.
They call a man to go with them!

The route here illustrated, northwards from
Sell Gill, is a typical packhorse road, a carpet
of soft luxury, heading purposefully for its
destination, in this case Langstrothdale, in
upper Wharfedale. An added interest is given
to this walk by the presence of several potholes
in the near vicinity of the track, and these may
conveniently be inspected from a safe distance :
they are dangerous, obviously so, frightening to
some people, fascinating to others.
Sell Gill Holes, with an entrance on each side of a
natural bridge carrying the road, is the best-known
of the series, engulfing a stream and opening into
a huge underground chamber 210 feet deep.
Jackdaw Hole is an open chasm enclosed by a wall.
Cowskull Pot, in a hollow, is a small shaft of 70 feet deep.
Penyghent Long Churn, 180 feet deep, swallows a stream.
Canal Cavern opens from an insignificant rift by the track.

A delightful green road

Hull Pot

The gritstone cap of Penyghent is succeeded by a dull moorland, on the descent to Horton, until surface limestone is reached at the contour of 1300'. Here is a 'classic' pothole area, and although several of the apertures are inconspicuous the two best known, Hull Pot and Hunt Pot — widely different in character — are readily located and may be visited with little loss of time. Hull Pot is an open chasm of remarkable size, 300' long, 60' wide and 60' deep; the waterfall, illustrated in the drawing, occurs only after heavy rainstorms, the stream normally sinking into its bed before reaching the pot. Hunt Pot is an evil slit, 15' long, 6' wide, and 200' deep, engulfing a stream. Both holes are enclosed by post and wire fencing and their dangers are obvious. The disappearing waters emerge from caves at Douk Gill Scar and Brants Gill Head near Horton.

Hunt Pot

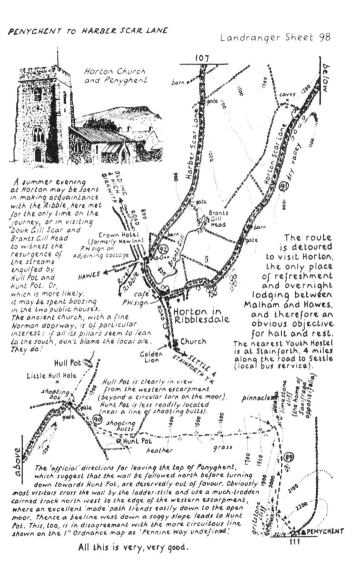

Horton Church and Penyghent

107

barn

gate

1100

below

1200

caves

dry valley

Harber Scar Lane

Horton Scar Lane

1000

OLD INC HIGH ROAD WITH DIRKWITH

800

gate

Brants Gill Head

barn

gate

Crown Hotel (formerly New Inn) PW sign on adjoining cottage

92

barn

Brants Gill

HAWES

River Ribble

café PW sign

Horton in Ribblesdale

ROAD

Church

Golden Lion

SETTLE & STAINFORTH Y.H.

A summer evening at Horton may be spent in making acquaintance with the Ribble, here met for the only time on the journey, or in visiting Douk Gill Scar and Brants Gill Head to witness the resurgence of the streams engulfed by Hull Pot and Hunt Pot. Or, which is more likely, it may be spent boozing in the two public houses. The ancient church, with a fine Norman doorway, is of particular interest: if all its pillars seem to lean to the south, don't blame the local ale. They do!

The route is detoured to visit Horton, the only place of refreshment and overnight lodging between Malham and Hawes, and therefore an obvious objective for halt and rest. The nearest Youth Hostel is at Stainforth, 4 miles along the road to Settle (local bus service).

Hull Pot

Little Hull Hole ×

shooting box ×

gate

90

shooting butts

Hunt Pot

heather

grass

Hull Pot is clearly in view from the western escarpment (beyond a circular tarn on the moor). Hunt Pot is less readily located (near a line of shooting butts).

above

1200

1700

1500

1600

1700 1800

pinnacles

limestone cliff (the home of Saxifraga opposit[ifol]ia)

1900 2000

89

gritstone cliff

2100

2200

stile

PENYGHENT

111

The 'official' directions for leaving the top of Penyghent, which suggest that the wall be followed north before turning down towards Hunt Pot, are deservedly out of favour. Obviously most visitors cross the wall by the ladder-stile and use a much-trodden cairned track north-west to the edge of the western escarpment, where an excellent 'made' path trends easily down to the open moor. Thence a beeline west down a soggy slope leads to Hunt Pot. This, too, is in disagreement with the more circuitous line shown on the 1" Ordnance map as 'Pennine Way undefined.'

All this is very, very good.

YORKSHIRE (W.R.)

Penyghent

Like all popular summits, Penyghent is a dump for litter, some of it (bottles, tins, plastic bags) being dangerous for sheep —which have far more right to enjoy Penyghent than ill-mannered humans.

Saxifraga oppositifolia

April visitors will ever afterwards remember Penyghent as the mountain of the purple saxifrage, for in April this beautiful plant decorates the white limestone cliffs on the 1900' contour with vivid splashes of colour, especially being rampant along the western cliff (overlooking the descent to Hunt Pot), which it drapes like aubretia on a garden wall.

The southern aspect

Striated rocks, gritstone cliff, south ridge.

Dale Head Farm

FOUNTAINS FELL TO PENYGHENT

The Ordnance Survey prefer to hyphenate the name PENYGHENT into PEN-Y-GHENT and will have good reason for doing so: hyphens here, as elsewhere, are an irritation, right or wrong. They also prefer to add the suffix 'Hill', but this detracts from a fine name and is never used in conversation. Walkers talk of PENYGHENT, not of PEN-Y-GHENT HILL.

Above the gritstone rockstep, the summit is reached alongside the wall on beautiful turf (or a short cut in rougher grass may be used). There is nothing exciting in the immediate vicinity of the cairn and the main interest lies in the excellent all-round view, which, clockwise from Fountains Fell, includes Pendle Hill and the Bowland Fells, lofty Ingleborough (looking noble, as usual), sprawling Whernside (hiding most of the Lakeland peaks), the shapely Howgill Fells and the shapeless Baugh Fell, Wildboar Fell with its cutaway right profile, the flat-topped Great Shunner Fell (the next summit on the Pennine Way) seen over Dodd Fell, Lovely Seat, and the heights bordering Wensleydale and Wharfedale.

The route from the road to Churn Milk Hole is plain sailing through a region of pleasant limestone outcrops past Dale Head Farm. At the Hole (which is a disappointment for eager explorers) a thin track leaves the wide Horton path (an old road, really) and heads north to join the south ridge of Penyghent at a stile in a corner of walls. Penyghent now looks very imposing, its two tiers of crags being much in evidence, but they do not bar the way up to the summit: the path climbs through weaknesses in the rocks and has no difficulties.

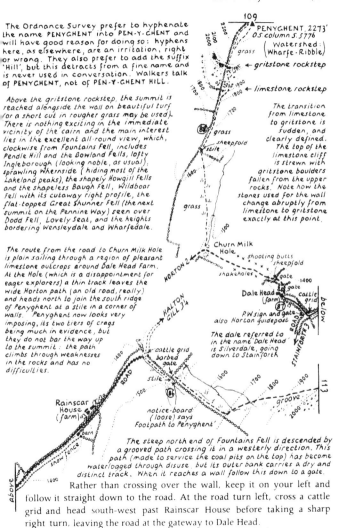

PENYGHENT, 2273'
OS column S.5776
(Watershed:
Wharfe-Ribble)
← gritstone rockstep
← limestone rockstep

The transition from limestone to gritstone is sudden, and clearly defined. The top of the limestone cliff is strewn with gritstone boulders fallen from the upper rocks. Note how the stones used for the wall change abruptly from limestone to gritstone exactly at this point.

Churn Milk Hole
shooting butts
sheepfold
shakeholes
gate
Dale Head (farm)
cattle grid
gate
P.W. sign and gate
also Horton guidepost

The dale referred to in the name 'Dale Head' is Silverdale, going down to Stainforth.

cattle grid
barbed gate
stile
Rainscar House (farm)
barn

notice-board (loose) says 'Footpath to Penyghent'

groove

The steep north end of Fountains Fell is descended by a grooved path crossing it in a westerly direction. This path (made to service the coal pits on the top) has become waterlogged through disuse, but its outer bank carries a dry and distinct track. When it reaches a wall follow this down to a gate.

Rather than crossing over the wall, keep it on your left and follow it straight down to the road. At the road turn left, cross a cattle grid and head south-west past Rainscar House before taking a sharp right turn, leaving the road at the gateway to Dale Head.

Map revised 1994.

A real mountain, at last.

YORKSHIRE (W.R)

The two stone men,
Fountains Fell.

Tennant Gill Farm

The top of Fountains Fell is gently undulating and very extensive. It is remarkable as the site of ancient coal mines, the ground over a wide area being pitted with old shafts. now filled in. A single building, 12 feet square, remains; the interior, shaped like an igloo, can be entered on the north side by crawling through a low arch. Two stone men (tall cairns) are conspicuously in view in the later stages of the approach from Tennant Gill.

The summit, 2191', with a large cairn, is a third of a mile distant to the south-west, and only slightly higher than the path across the top. A strange landscape! The name of the fell is derived from Fountains Abbey, the landowners centuries ago.

The 'igloo'

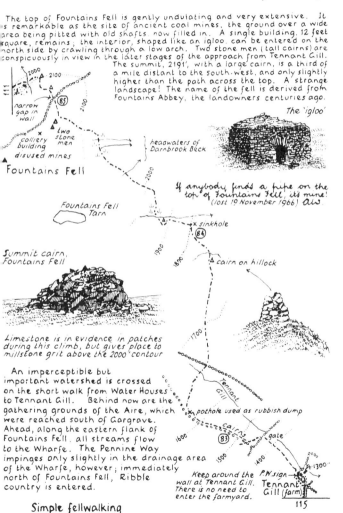

If anybody finds a pipe on the top of Fountains Fell, its mine! (lost 19 November 1966) AW

Limestone is in evidence, in patches during this climb, but gives place to millstone grit above the 2000' contour

Fountains Fell
Fountains Fell Tarn
Summit cairn, Fountains Fell

An imperceptible but important watershed is crossed on the short walk from Water Houses to Tennant Gill. Behind now are the gathering grounds of the Aire, which were reached south of Gargrave. Ahead, along the eastern flank of Fountains Fell, all streams flow to the Wharfe. The Pennine Way impinges only slightly in the drainage area of the Wharfe, however; immediately north of Fountains Fell, Ribble country is entered.

Keep around the wall at Tennant Gill. There is no need to enter the farmyard.

P.W.sign
Tennant Gill (farm)

Simple fellwalking

YORKSHIRE (W.R.)

Malham Tarn House

One's first reaction on seeing Malham Tarn House is of wonderment that such a splendid mansion should ever have been built here, in this particular location, miles from anywhere and in the middle of a bleak tableland 1350' above sea level. The site was originally occupied by a shooting lodge, which seems more appropriate to the surroundings, the present house being built over a century ago as a private residence: as such it enjoyed visits from many literary celebrities. Charles Kingsley's 'Water Babies' was inspired by the scenery. Shorn of some of its original ornate features, in particular a tower in the east wing, the property with its extensive grounds is now owned by the National Trust and used as a centre by the Council for Promotion of Field Studies. The natural life of the area is preserved and protected, the resident staff catering for groups of students and other interested visitors. Formerly the environs of Malham Tarn were unfrequented and almost unknown outside the locality, but now, on any summer weekend, the place attracts many people in sympathy with the Council's objects and there is much pedestrian activity in the woods, on the paths and by the shore, cars happily being prohibited from the reserve. *Once a shooting lodge for the destruction of birds, now a sanctuary for their preservation.* A gleam of hope for the human race, too!

Malham Tarn

Malham Tarn is a surprise. All around are the gleaming white cliffs and outcrops of limestone, and limestone, being porous, does not hold surface water, hence the labyrinth of subterranean passages, caves and potholes honeycombing the underworld of limestone country. Yet Malham Tarn is not only permanent but extensive, measuring roughly half-a-mile square. The explanation is geological, that it lies on a bed of harder rock, Silurian slate, which is impervious to water and recurs in patches along the line of the disturbance, the North Craven Fault, that influences the landscape hereabouts. The tarn is a sanctuary for birds and waterfowl, which enjoy here a life free from persecution.

MALHAM TARN TO TENNANT GILL

Landranger Sheet 98

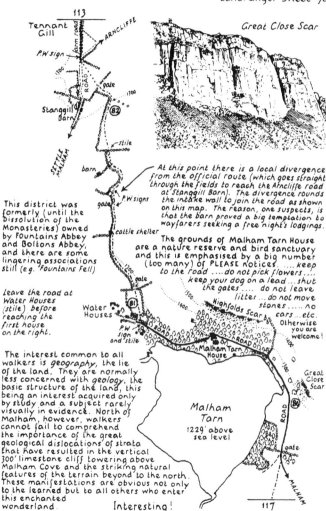

Great Close Scar

Tennant Gill

113

ARNCLIFFE

farm road

P.W sign

1700

ROAD

gate

1700

82

Stanggill Barn

SETTLE — MALHAM

stile

barn

P.W signs

gate

At this point there is a local divergence from the official route (which goes straight through the fields to reach the Arncliffe road at Stanggill Barn). The divergence rounds the intake wall to join the road as shown on this map. The reason, one suspects, is that the barn proved a big temptation to wayfarers seeking a free night's lodging.

This district was formerly (until the Dissolution of the Monasteries) owned by Fountains Abbey and Boltons Abbey, and there are some lingering associations still (e.g. 'Fountains Fell')

cattle shelter

The grounds of Malham Tarn House are a nature reserve and bird sanctuary and this is emphasised by a big number (too many) of PLEASE notices. ....keep to the road ....do not pick flowers.... keep your dog on a lead ...shut the gates.... do not leave litter ...do not move stones .....no cars .....etc. Otherwise you are welcome!

1300

gate

Leave the road at Water Houses (stile) before reaching the first house on the right.

Water Houses

81

1400

Highfolds Scar

ROAD

P.W sign and stile

ROAD

Malham Tarn House

The interest common to all walkers is geography, the lie of the land. They are normally less concerned with geology, the basic structure of the land, this being an interest acquired only by study and a subject rarely visually in evidence. North of Malham, however, walkers cannot fail to comprehend the importance of the great geological dislocations of strata that have resulted in the vertical 300' limestone cliff towering above Malham Cove and the striking natural features of terrain beyond to the north. These manifestations are obvious not only to the learned but to all others who enter this enchanted wonderland.

Malham Tarn
1229' above sea level

Great Close Scar

84

ROAD

gate

MALHAM

Interesting!

117

Map slightly amended 1994.

Malham Cove

MALHAM TO MALHAM TARN

Water Sinks

The official P.W. route crosses the depression beyond the limestone pavement and climbs the opposite slope to join a path that runs north through the miniature ravine of Trougate and across the open moor of Prior Rakes to the Malham Moor road. Much more interesting is the 'unofficial' route up and out of the Dry Valley to Water Sinks, rejoining the main route along the road. Dry Valley is a fine example of Ice Age erosion. The exit from its floor below Comb Hill is not obvious and may be missed: note the sharp zig-zag necessary to gain its continuation above an 80' dry waterfall on the right. A cave here gives good shelter. The rest is easy.

The limestone country around Malham is the best walkers' territory so far encountered along the Pennine Way, and there is nothing better to come. Green tracks, rich turf and strangely beautiful scenery make Malham an ideal centre for a lengthy exploration. A booklet "Malhamdale" by Dr. A. Raistrick (Dalesman Publishing Co. Ltd) is an excellent and informative guide to this charming district.

Above the Cove is an extensive area of limestone pavement, fissured and contorted like a brain. Walk very carefully here, or avoid it around the fringe: it has unique propensities for breaking legs. The unprotected edge of the cliff is especially dangerous. But visit the lowest part of the rim, where once poured a waterfall higher than Niagara.

Malhamdale is rich in its evidences of the occupation of prehistoric man. The fields crossed between Malham and the Cove bear indications of ancient enclosures, not well seen at ground level but distinct when viewed aerially. Look back over the line of approach from the rim of Malham Cove and the ridged pattern of the enclosures and cultivation terraces is clearly delineated.

Malham Beck issues silently from an impenetrable slit at the base of the cliff at Malham Cove. This is the return to daylight of a stream that sinks underground near the ruins of an old smelt mill on the moor above, 1½ miles northwest.

At Water Sinks the stream issuing from Malham Tarn vanishes quietly underground at a junction of walls: this is the stream that re-appears at Aire Head Springs, south of Malham — NOT the stream that emerges in Malham Cove as might be supposed (proved by chemical tests)

Fascinating!

YORKSHIRE (W.R.)

left : the gorge

Gordale
Scar

below :
the waterfalls

If the detour to Gordale Scar is made, Janet's Foss, a pretty waterfall in a perfect setting, should be visited too — it is conveniently reached from the road to the Scar, by a path opposite the ruin of a barn, but is more pleasantly approached upstream in the lovely dell of Gordale Beck, a route strongly recommended (see map opposite for route)

Janet's Foss

Landranger Sheets 103 and 98

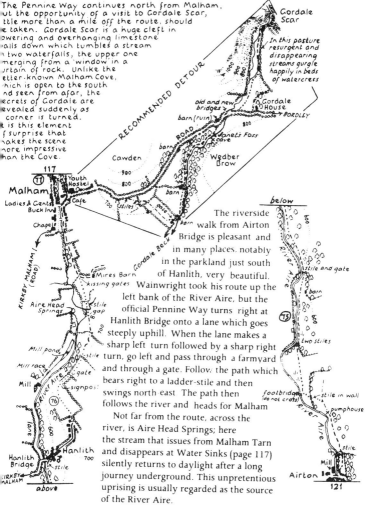

The Pennine Way continues north from Malham, but the opportunity of a visit to Gordale Scar, little more than a mile off the route, should be taken. Gordale Scar is a huge cleft in towering and overhanging limestone walls down which tumbles a stream in two waterfalls, the upper one emerging from a 'window' in a curtain of rock. Unlike the better-known Malham Cove, which is open to the south and seen from afar, the secrets of Gordale are revealed suddenly as a corner is turned. It is this element of surprise that makes the scene more impressive than the Cove.

RECOMMENDED DETOUR

Gordale Scar

In this pasture resurgent and disappearing streams gurgle happily in beds of watercress

old and new bridges

Gordale House

TO BORDLEY

barn (ruin)

ROAD

Janet's Foss cave

barn

Wedber Brow

Cawden

900

117

Malham

Youth Hostel

800

Ladies & Gents

Buck Inn

Cafe

Chapel

700 stiles

gate

barn

KIRBY MALHAM (ROAD)

Cordale Beck

Mires Barn

kissing gates

Aire Head Springs

stile gap

Mill pond

stile

Mill race

gate

Mill

signpost

76

Hanlith

Hanlith Bridge

stile

KIRKBY MALHAM

700

above

below

river Aire

stile and gate

barn

79

two stiles

footbridge (do not cross)

stile in wall

pumphouse

river Aire

stile

Mill

Airton

121

The riverside walk from Airton Bridge is pleasant and in many places, notably in the parkland just south of Hanlith, very beautiful. Wainwright took his route up the left bank of the River Aire, but the official Pennine Way turns right at Hanlith Bridge onto a lane which goes steeply uphill. When the lane makes a sharp left turn followed by a sharp right turn, go left and pass through a farmyard and through a gate. Follow the path which bears right to a ladder-stile and then swings north east. The path then follows the river and heads for Malham

Not far from the route, across the river, is Aire Head Springs; here the stream that issues from Malham Tarn and disappears at Water Sinks (page 117) silently returns to daylight after a long journey underground. This unpretentious uprising is usually regarded as the source of the River Aire.

Map revised 1994.

Enjoyable and exciting

3 Bridges over the Aire

Airton Bridge

Newfield Bridge

Footbridge below Newfield Bridge

GARGRAVE TO AIRTON

Landranger Sheet 103

across

Eshton Moor

119

Airton

CALTON

74

telephone poles

pond

72

Haw Crag
× 0.5 column

gate

B

gate

stiles

500

gate

Newfield Laithe
quarry

Laithe (= barn)
is a common name
in this district.
In the old quarry near
Newfield Laithe there
are signs of intense
foldings in the thin
limestone strata.

AIRTON

Newfield Bridge

stile

Newfield
Hall

stile

stile

River Aire

ROAD

gate

C

500

A

gate

Horrows
Hill

13

Beyond the plantation
on Horrows Hill the
Pennine Way is
prevented from making
a beeline from A to B
(as it is supposed to do)
by barbed-wire fences.
Instead aim for a gate
in the wall (C) and
continue alongside.

stile

footbridge

stile
P.W.sign

500

ESHTON

pastures

across

71

BELL BUSK
(lane)

At the far end of Mark
Plantation, the road (now
deteriorating into a lane) is
left either by a narrow gate
into a thistly field, or by a wider
one 100 yards further. Another gate
near Middle Plantation gives access to
a rising slope up to Horrows Hill through
a pasture rich with beef on the hoof. It
was here that the author unknowingly
passed close to a bull with a ring in its nose
(a circumstance reported by an interested and
disappointed spectator): this was not courage,
but myopia. Well, they say the devil looks after
his own.
There is no recognisable path until Eshton Moor
is reached, and little evidence of use.

gates

Mark
Plantation

400

barn

P.W.sign

Leave Gargrave along West Street (note the
P.W.sign under the street name-plate). Over
the canal bridge the road is flanked by noble
trees in pleasant park-like surroundings.

Gargrave
House

canal

Gargrave

SETTLE 103

ROAD
A.65

R. Aire

70

Through green pastures

123

Double Arched Bridge, East Marton, carrying the busy A.59 road
over the Leeds and Liverpool Canal.
Why the top arch? Obviously it was never intended to accommodate
the canal. Think about it. The clue is given in the caption *in italics.*

East Marton Church

Stone-slab footbridge, Langber Beck

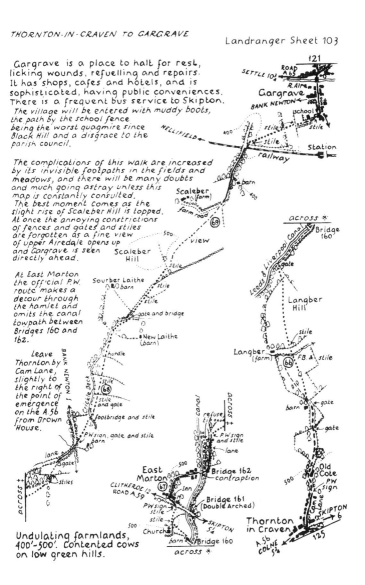

THORNTON·IN·CRAVEN TO GARGRAVE

Landranger Sheet 103

Gargrave is a place to halt for rest, licking wounds, refuelling and repairs. It has shops, cafés and hotels, and is sophisticated, having public conveniences. There is a frequent bus service to Skipton.

The village will be entered with muddy boots, the path by the school fence being the worst quagmire since Black Hill and a disgrace to the parish council.

The complications of this walk are increased by its invisible footpaths in the fields and meadows, and there will be many doubts and much going astray unless this map is constantly consulted.

The best moment comes as the slight rise of Scaleber Hill is topped. At once the annoying constrictions of fences and gates and stiles are forgotten as a fine view of upper Airedale opens up and Gargrave is seen directly ahead.

At East Marton the official P.W. route makes a detour through the hamlet and omits the canal towpath between Bridges 160 and 162.

Leave Thornton by Cam Lane, slightly to the right of the point of emergence on the A.56 from Brown House.

Undulating farmlands, 400'–500'. Contented cows on low green hills.

Map labels

SETTLE 10¾ ROAD A.65 121

Gargrave

BANK NEWTON

school

stile   stile

HELLIFIELD

400

stile

stile

Station

railway

barn

400

Scaleber (farm)

farm road

across ✳

Bridge 160

69

500

view

Leeds & Liverpool Canal

gate

Scaleber Hill

stile

Langber Hill

Sourber Laithe (barn)

stile

stile

gate and bridge

stile

New Laithe (barn)

Langber (farm)   FB.   stile

66

dip

hurdle

BANK NEWTON

Cam Beck

stile

68

barn   gate

stile and gate

footbridge and stile

gate

across ✳

canal

refuse tip area

P.W.sign, gate and stile   barn

P.W.sign and stile

lane

lane

gate

stiles

across

East Marton   500

Bridge 162 contraption

67

Inn

CLITHEROE 12   ROAD A.59

P.W.sign stile

Bridge 161 (Double Arched)

barn

Church

500   SKIPTON 5¼

Bridge 160

across ✳

Old Cote

P.W. sign

500

SKIPTON 6

Thornton in Craven   125

A.56 COLNE 5¼

Pinhaw Beacon

Despite all the attention to detail in the planning of the route of the Pennine Way prior to its official recognition, it was inevitable that, in the early years following, local doubts and disputes would arise in some approved sections. Many such cases have arisen, one example being the route across Pinhaw Moor, where complaints by walkers that the 'right of way' was being questioned by the shooting tenant and a misleading notice erected were remedied by the joint action of the National Parks Commission and the County Council at the instigation of the Ramblers' Association. In other cases, farmers have made minor variations to the approved route, doing their own signposting, but where this is necessary to prevent damage or disturbance to growing crops or property there can be little quarrel with their action.
Not all walkers are saints. Some are damn nuisances.

Lothersdale

LOTHERSDALE TO THORNTON-IN-CRAVEN

Landranger Sheet 103

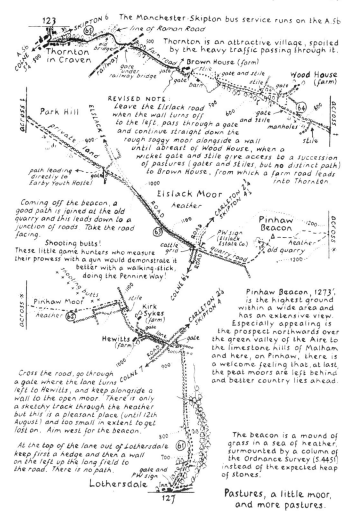

The Manchester-Skipton bus service runs on the A.56

line of Roman Road

Thornton is an attractive village, spoiled by the heavy traffic passing through it.

123

SKIPTON 6

A.56 COLNE 53 500

Thornton in Craven

railway

gate under railway bridge

old bridge

500

farm road

gate gate

gate

barn

Brown House (farm)

gate and stile

stile

stile

gate

Wood House (farm)

Park Hill

EISLACK

private land

900

path leading directly to Earby Youth Hostel

gate

REVISED NOTE:
Leave the Eislack road when the wall turns off to the left, pass through a gate and continue straight down the rough soggy moor alongside a wall until abreast of Wood House, when a wicket gate and stile give access to a succession of pastures (gates and stiles, but no distinct path) to Brown House, from which a farm road leads into Thornton.

500 600

gate and stile

64

across →

manholes

stile

1000

Eislack Moor

heather

CARLETON 2¼ SKIPTON 4¼

Pinhaw Beacon

1200

across →

heather

1100

Coming off the beacon, a good path is joined at the old quarry and this leads down to a junction of roads. Take the road facing.

Shooting butts!
These little game hunters who measure their prowess with a gun would demonstrate it better with a walking-stick, doing the Pennine Way!

63

ROAD

cattle grid

PW sign (Eislack Estate Co)

quarry road

old quarry

1200

1000

Shooting butts

Pinhaw Moor

heather

62

stile

Kirk Sykes (farm)

gate

lane

Hewitts (farm)

gate

COLNE 6½

CARLETON 2¼ SKIPTON 4¼

Pinhaw Beacon, 1273', is the highest ground within a wide area and has an extensive view. Especially appealing is the prospect northwards over the green valley of the Aire to the limestone hills of Malham and here, on Pinhaw, there is a welcome feeling that, at last, the peat moors are left behind and better country lies ahead.

1000

ROAD

COLNE 7

900

Cross the road, go through a gate where the lane turns left to Hewitts, and keep alongside a wall to the open moor. There is only a sketchy track through the heather but this is a pleasant place (until 12th August) and too small in extent to get lost on. Aim west for the beacon.

At the top of the lane out of Lothersdale keep first a hedge and then a wall on the left up the long field to the road. There is no path.

800

61

700

gate and PW sign

Lothersdale

Inn

127

The beacon is a mound of grass in a sea of heather, surmounted by a column of the Ordnance Survey (S.4451) instead of the expected heap of stones.

Pastures, a little moor, and more pastures.

A corner of old Lothersdale

Ruins of the old mill, Gill Bridge

Cowling Parish Church

Local bus service to Crosshills (for Skipton or Keighley)

ROAD 125 →CROSSHILLS 3
COLNE 7
Lin.
Mill
Lothersdale
700
800
farm road
700

Wood Head (farm)
gate
overgrown lane
gate Surgill Beck
gate
60
700
gate
stile
MILL CLOSE
800

Almost opposite the Hare and Hounds is a small car park bordering Lothersdale Beck, to which steps lead down. The beck here flows into a tunnel beneath the mill, and formerly operated a water-wheel, which has been preserved although not now in use. This part of the village is delightful.

Lothersdale comes into view suddenly after topping the hill beyond Wood Head, a pleasant and picturesque grouping of old cottages and a textile mill, so deeply inurned in its wooded valley that, from this viewpoint, the beholder looks down into the top of the mill chimney. It is even better on closer acquaintance, many of the old houses being interesting and distinctive. An inn and a shop further contribute to the joys of Lothersdale.

Lothersdale is friendly, as few places on the Pennine Way are, and here, for the first time since leaving Edale, most walkers will feel a reluctance to proceed and a temptation to linger and enjoy the peaceful hospitality of the place. If Black Hill and Redmires Moss were necessary to discover the charms of eventide and early morning in Lothersdale they were worth it. A pity it can be reached by car!

900
ROAD
ROAD
gate ROAD →COWLING HILL
1000

On this gentle climb there is a good view back across Cowling to the two monuments on the skyline of Earl Crag.

gateway
900
stile barn and untenanted cottages
gate
gate and stile
800 stile
hen huts
59 stiles
700
ruin gates and stiles
OX Gill Beck
Gill Bridge

Gill Lane is notable only for its ugly lines of poles, but Gill Bridge is set in a charming wooded dell. Turn left here. Note the ruins: mullioned windows lying around suggest a building of character. In the rear is a dry mill-pond.

Middleton is a curious street of terraced houses —an industrial offshoot of an age gone by.

Upon reaching the A6808, Labour Party members may feel a duty to proceed east along it, for a third of a mile, to see a tree planted in memory of Lord (Philip) Snowden of Ickornshaw. Conservatives and Liberals should turn left, and then right just before the Black Bull; then right into the village street of Ickornshaw, and left at a building that used to be a chapel. The route goes past houses and along the edge of a field, passing on the right the curious street of terraced houses called Middleton. Follow a wall, then turn right through the wall to turn left into Gill Lane.

spring
Middleton
School
Cowling Parish Church
KEIGHLEY 7½
Ladies & Gents
Ickornshaw
700 Mill
COLNE 5½
Bus service ROAD A6808
129

Map revised 1994.

Waterfall,
Lumb Head Beck

Wainman's
Pinnacle

Lund's
Tower

The Monuments on Earl Crag

Earl Crag, an abrupt rampart of gritstone overlooking Cowling, is not on the route of the Pennine Way, but its two conspicuous monuments attract the attention during the long descent of Ickornshaw Moor.

Here they are, as seen at close range. For anyone staying overnight in the vicinity, a visit to them makes a pleasant evening stroll. Go up the Oakworth road.

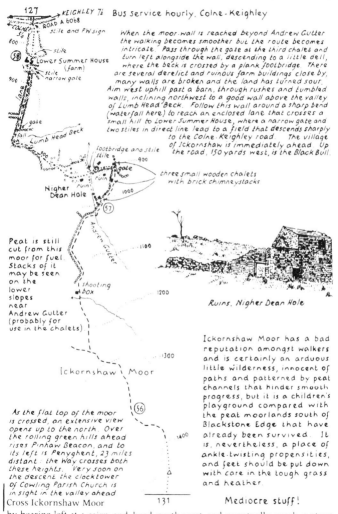

127 KEIGHLEY 7½ Bus service hourly. Colne - Keighley

When the moor wall is reached beyond Andrew Gutter the walking becomes smoother but the route becomes intricate. Pass through the gate at the third chalet and turn left alongside the wall, descending to a little dell, where the beck is crossed by a plank footbridge. There are several derelict and ruinous farm buildings close by, many walls are broken and the land has turned sour. Aim west uphill past a barn, through rushes and tumbled walls, inclining northwest to a good wall above the valley of Lumb Head Beck. Follow this wall around a sharp bend (waterfall here) to reach an enclosed lane that crosses a small hill to Lower Summer House, where a narrow gate and two stiles in direct line lead to a field that descends sharply to the Colne-Keighley road. The village of Ickornshaw is immediately ahead. Up the road, 150 yards west, is the Black Bull.

three small wooden chalets with brick chimneystacks

Peat is still cut from this moor for fuel. Stacks of it may be seen on the lower slopes near Andrew Gutter (probably for use in the chalets).

Ruins, Nigher Dean Hole

Ickornshaw Moor has a bad reputation amongst walkers and is certainly an arduous little wilderness, innocent of paths and patterned by peat channels that hinder smooth progress, but it is a children's playground compared with the peat moorlands south of Blackstone Edge that have already been survived. It is, nevertheless, a place of ankle-twisting propensities, and feet should be put down with care in the tough grass and heather.

As the flat top of the moor is crossed, an extensive view opens up to the north. Over the rolling green hills ahead rises Pinhaw Beacon, and to its left is Penyghent, 23 miles distant: the Way crosses both these heights. Very soon on the descent the clocktower of Cowling Parish Church is in sight in the valley ahead

Mediocre stuff!

Cross Ickornshaw Moor by bearing left at a cairn and head north-west and eventually reach a stone shelter. Continue northwards to join a path beside a wall leading down to Andrew Gutter.

Map revised 1994.

YORKSHIRE (W.R.)

*An abandoned farmhouse
near Ponden Reservoir*

Derelict and ruinous farmbuildings
are a sad but unfortunately a common
feature of the Yorkshire moors, especially in
the industrial West Riding.   Many of them were
originally houses of substance and character, but with the passing of the years
they fell victims to cruel circumstance. Changing economic conditions brought
disaster to the small hill farmer; in some cases
new reservoirs needed for the growing towns
swallowed his land. Proud men once lived on
these farms; now they are left to their ghosts.

Ponden Hall

WITHINS TO WOLF STONES

Landranger Sheet 103

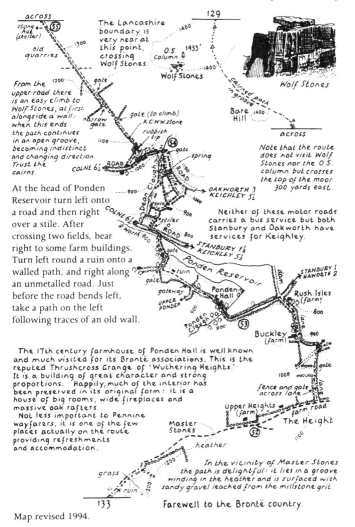

across

stone hut (shelter)
old quarries
55
1300

The Lancashire boundary is very near at this point, crossing Wolf Stones.

129

1400

O.S. 1455'
column

1400

Wolf Stones

Wolf Stones

cairned path in groove

From the upper road there is an easy climb to Wolf Stones, at first alongside a wall: when this ends the path continues in an open groove, becoming indistinct and changing direction. Trust the cairns.

1200
gate

narrow gate

gate (to climb)
K.C.W.W.stone
rubbish tip

1100

54
gate
spring

ROAD

COLNE 6½

1000

ROAD

Bare Hill *1400*

across

Note that the route does not visit Wolf Stones nor the O.S. column but crosses the top of the moor 300 yards east.

At the head of Ponden Reservoir turn left onto a road and then right over a stile. After crossing two fields, bear right to some farm buildings. Turn left round a ruin onto a walled path, and right along an unmetalled road. Just before the road bends left, take a path on the left following traces of an old wall.

Dean Clough

900

COLNE 6½

Worth
800

900

stiles

800

ROAD

OAKWORTH 3
KEIGHLEY 5½

Neither of these motor roads carries a bus service but both Stanbury and Oakworth have services for Keighley.

STANBURY 1½
KEIGHLEY 5½

gate

Ponden Reservoir

ruin

gateway

UPPER PONDEN

Ponden Hall

Ponden Clough
800

53

STANBURY 1
HAWORTH 2

dam

Rush Isles (farm)

800

Buckley (farm)

900

1000

gate

fence and gate across lane

The 17th century farmhouse of Ponden Hall is well known and much visited for its Brontë associations. This is the reputed Thrushcross Grange of 'Wuthering Heights.' It is a building of great character and strong proportions. Happily, much of the interior has been preserved in its original form: it is a house of big rooms, wide fireplaces and massive oak rafters.

Not less important to Pennine wayfarers, it is one of the few places actually on the route providing refreshments and accommodation.

Master Stones

Upper Heights (farm)
farm road
The Height

52

1100

heather

1200

grass

ruin
1200

133

In the vicinity of Master Stones the path is delightful: it lies in a groove winding in the heather and is surfaced with sandy gravel leached from the millstone grit.

Farewell to the Brontë country.

Map revised 1994.

Withins

Withins — a decayed skeleton of a house, with crumbled bones and sightless eyes, perched high on a desolate moor, windswept and ravaged by storms, forsaken, abandoned to nature, the walls of its fields broken and the grass grown coarse and rank with neglect.

Such is Withins today, in sad plight but not different from a hundred other ruinous moorland farmhouses high on the Pennines. But public imagination, inspired by the novel of Emily Brontë, has long regarded Withins as her Wuthering Heights, and it has become a place of pilgrimage. The setting is grim, austere, a lonely dwelling in a wasteland of heather and peat.   In its day Withins must have been a house of good appearance, as the dressed stones and mullions and buttresses still testify, but that day has gone.   Only the ghosts of the past find shelter here now, and only the few trees show life.

TOP WITHENS.

THIS FARMHOUSE HAS BEEN ASSOCIATED WITH
" WUTHERING HEIGHTS "
THE EARNSHAW HOME IN EMILY BRONTË'S
NOVEL.
THE BUILDINGS, EVEN WHEN COMPLETE, BORE
NO RESEMBLANCE TO THE HOUSE SHE
DESCRIBED,
BUT THE SITUATION MAY HAVE BEEN IN HER
MIND WHEN SHE WROTE OF THE MOORLAND
SETTING OF THE HEIGHTS.

BRONTË SOCIETY   THIS PLAQUE HAS BEEN PLACED HERE
1964   IN RESPONSE TO MANY INQUIRIES.

The plaque on the wall

That Withins is a place of popular resort is evident from the scattered litter, the defaced walls, and a lot of wanton damage.   Not all of its visitors go there out of respect for Emily Brontë.

WITHINS is the spelling used on Ordnance maps. WITHENS is the spelling preferred locally.

Withins in 1967

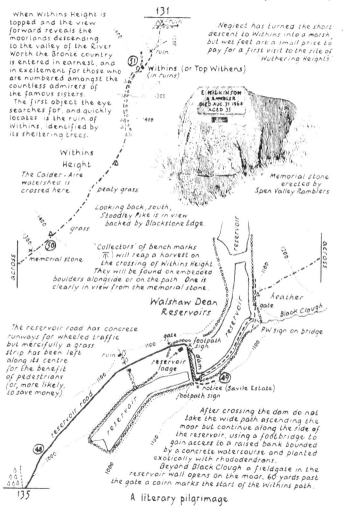

When Withins Height is topped and the view forward reveals the moorlands descending to the valley of the River Worth the Brontë country is entered in earnest, and in excitement for those who are numbered amongst the countless admirers of the famous sisters.

The first object the eye searches for, and quickly locates is the ruin of Withins, identified by its sheltering trees.

Withins Height

The Calder-Aire watershed is crossed here.

Neglect has turned the short descent to Withins into a marsh, but wet feet are a small price to pay for a first visit to the site of 'Wuthering Heights'

E. WILKINSON
RAMBLER
DIED AUG 3ⁿ 1964
AGED 35

Memorial stone
erected by
Spen Valley Ramblers

Withins (or Top Withins)
(in ruins)

✕ ruin
ruin

peaty grass

Looking back, south, Stoodley Pike is in view backed by Blackstone Edge.

grass

'Collectors' of bench marks ⊼ will reap a harvest on the crossing of Withins Height. They will be found on embedded boulders alongside or on the path. One is clearly in view from the memorial stone.

memorial stone

across

Walshaw Dean Reservoirs

reservoir

reservoir

reservoir

heather
gate
Black Clough

PW sign on bridge

The reservoir road has concrete runways for wheeled traffic but mercifully a grass strip has been left along its centre for the benefit of pedestrians (or, more likely, to save money).

reservoir road

reservoir

gate
footpath sign

ruin

reservoir lodge

dam

✕ notice (Savile Estate)
footpath sign

After crossing the dam do not take the wide path ascending the moor but continue along the side of the reservoir, using a footbridge to gain access to a raised bank bounded by a concrete watercourse and planted exotically with rhododendrons.
Beyond Black Clough a fieldgate in the reservoir wall opens on the moor. 60 yards past the gate a cairn marks the start of the Withins path.

A literary pilgrimage

The Hebden Bridge district

On the walk over Clough Head Hill to the Colne road, and in lesser degree earlier, from the heights south of Colden, a deep wooded valley running east of the route attracts the eye of the traveller. It looks good. And it is good, so good that it seems a pity that the Pennine Way should prefer to bypass it. This is the valley of Hebden Water, several miles of steep-sided rocky gorge richly adorned with trees, containing in its shadows the pleasant stream and many charming public footpaths. More often referred to as Hardcastle Crags, this valley has long been known to Lancashire and Yorkshire people as an idyllic retreat far removed in scenic quality from the grim environment of the industrial towns. 'The Switzerland of the North' it was named in older days, and excursion trains brought to Hebden Bridge Station hundreds of visitors every summer weekend. Hebden Bridge itself, a small manufacturing town, has little to commend it as a place of beauty, but the arrangement of its buildings is strikingly attractive, especially when viewed from the steep roads dropping into it on the west side, its terraced stone houses rising in tiers out of the narrow throat of the valley after the style of a Tibetan monastery, far overtopping the industrial arteries of road, railway, river and canal, and dwarfing even the tall mill chimneys. This is a town of steep gradients and spiralling pedestrian alleys, and the wonder is that it has not produced a supply of Everest climbers. On a lofty perch overlooking the town is the conspicuous churchtower and quaint village of Heptonstall, a place with a proud history.

All other feeders of the River Calder in the vicinity and indeed the Calder itself exhibit the same characteristics, appearing as deep wooded clefts in the hills. Man has spoiled but not destroyed their charm and in the recesses where industry has not ventured it is still possible to appreciate the rare and unexpected beauty that once lay virgin in the folds of these barren Yorkshire moors. The Switzerland of the North: yes, before the area was exploited for brass the name must surely have been deserved.

Ancient
gateposts
and modern
footbridges,
Graining
Water

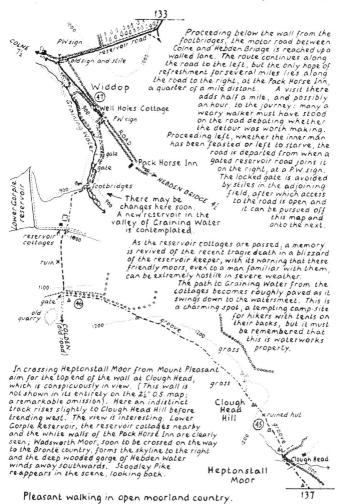

HEPTONSTALL MOOR TO WIDDOP

Landranger Sheet 103

133

COLNE 7½

PW sign

reservoir road

old sign and stile

Widdop

(47)

Well Holes Cottage

PW sign

ROAD

gate

gate

Pack Horse Inn

HEBDEN BRIDGE 4½

footbridges

Graining Water

Lower Gorple Reservoir

reservoir cottages

ruin ✕

gate

old quarry

(46)

COLDEN (old road)

1200

groove

1200

grass

1000

1100

900

1000

1100

Proceeding below the wall from the footbridges, the motor road between Colne and Hebden Bridge is reached up a walled lane. The route continues along the road to the left, but the only hope of refreshment for several miles lies along the road to the right, at the Pack Horse Inn, a quarter of a mile distant.   A visit there adds half a mile, and possibly an hour, to the journey: many a weary walker must have stood on the road debating whether the detour was worth making.

Proceeding left, whether the inner man has been feasted or left to starve, the road is departed from when a gated reservoir road joins it on the right, at a P.W. sign. The locked gate is avoided by stiles in the adjoining field, after which access to the road is open and it can be pursued off this map and onto the next.

→ There may be changes here soon. A new reservoir in the valley of Graining Water is contemplated.

As the reservoir cottages are passed, a memory is revived of the recent tragic death in a blizzard of the reservoir keeper, with its warning that these friendly moors, even to a man familiar with them, can be extremely hostile in severe weather.

The path to Graining Water from the cottages becomes roughly paved as it swings down to the watersmeet. This is a charming spot, a tempting camp-site for hikers with tents on their backs, but it must be remembered that this is waterworks property.

grass

grass

Clough Head Hill

✕ ruined hut

(45)

groove

1200

1100

Clough Head

Heptonstall Moor

137

In crossing Heptonstall Moor from Mount Pleasant aim for the top end of the wall at Clough Head, which is conspicuously in view. (This wall is not shown in its entirety on the 2½" O.S. map; a remarkable omission). Here an indistinct track rises slightly to Clough Head Hill before trending west. The view is interesting. Lower Gorple Reservoir, the reservoir cottages nearby and the white walls of the Pack Horse Inn are clearly seen; Wadsworth Moor, soon to be crossed on the way to the Brontë country, forms the skyline to the right and the deep wooded gorge of Hebden Water winds away southwards. Stoodley Pike re-appears in the scene, looking back.

Pleasant walking in open moorland country.

Footbridge, Colden Water

Footpaths in the Calder Valley

Footpaths are important to the walker: they are made for his benefit and they provide his means of progression. Often they are no more than trodden ways in the grass. But in the area of the map on the opposite page they are of unusual interest: hereabouts, in a rural district closely linked to an urban, examples are met of a type of footpath not found elsewhere on the Pennine Way. Obviously they date back to the time of the construction of the carriage roads, when there was as much concern for foot-travellers as for those with conveyances, and they were made with care in the form of narrow paved ways between enclosing stone walls.   Habits of travel have changed, and while the roads have been improved many of the footpaths have fallen into neglect: the walls have collapsed and the paved surfaces become overgrown watercourses. A few good examples remain, notably, on the route of the Pennine Way, the path rising from the railway in the Calder Valley.

The Calder Valley
looking east
from the ruined chapel

This section of the route is intricate, consisting of a lot of little bits linked together, and the following notes are given in full to supplement the map.

Read the notes downwards, the map upwards.

Leave the busy A 646 80 yards to the right of the point of arrival on it, on the opposite side of the road (mind you don't get knocked down crossing it), where a short side-street with a P.W sign passes under a railway bridge.

Shortly after crossing underneath the railway bridge, the track bears left and then pasture and a wood appear on the right. Just past a ruined building and before the ruined Mount Olivet Baptist Chapel, the new route turns sharp right at a Pennine Way sign. The route continues along the hillside on a level path, and then rises until some steps are reached at a point where there is a little waterfall in a square stone column. The path continues around some partially ruined farm buildings. Bear left and head for a gap in the wall on the right after 100 yards. At this point, the original route is rejoined heading north.

Now, for the first time since leaving the valley, the route is straight forward to the north, crossing a tarmac road and the small Pry Hill, a good viewpoint, before descending into the wooded dell of Colden Water, a pleasant spot. Over the stone footbridge, go downstream to a stile, then uphill northwards again to reach the Burnley-Slack-Hebden Bridge road alongside, surprisingly, a modern housing estate. Across the road is a narrow gate and at the top of the field another. Cross a rough road and follow a crumbling walled lane that climbs to the left, reaching open ground, at last, at Long High Top. Follow the right-hand wall, under an electricity cable, over the crest of the moor, where the prospect ahead is decidedly improved, until nearly opposite Mount Pleasant. Here strike across the moor north-north-west.

Map revised 1994.

YORKSHIRE (W.R.)

The road in Callis Wood

The spring,
Stoodley Pike

STOODLEY PIKE TO THE RIVER CALDER

Landranger Sheet 103

Arrival in the valley of the Calder marks a definite stage of the Pennine Way. Behind now are the lonely peat moors, a desolate and inhospitable region. Ahead for the next 30 miles is easier terrain: high country still at first, but with habitations and small communities on or near the route of the Way until it declines to the wide strath of the Aire, where the scenery is completely pastoral. Behind is the black earth. Ahead is greenery — and lots of cows. Behind is mud; ahead is manure. The next definite stage is reached at Malham, at the threshold of the limestone country and its strange and beautiful landscapes.

For the first time since Longdendale the Pennine Way comes down from the tops to cross a valley. The descent to the Calder, on a farm road, is beautifully wooded, but suddenly, and shockingly, the route emerges from the trees and the eye recoils from the industrial blight immediately in front — a stagnant canal, a dirty river, a busy road and a railway crowded side by side. So does the nose, for the point of emergence into this tangle of communications is between a pig farm and a sewage works. Mercifully the valley is narrow and the crossing brief: within two minutes it can be left behind. But if overnight accommodation is required a bus may be caught here for Hebden Bridge. The A.646, unlike the many roads so far crossed, which have all been trans-Pennine, is a valley road linking industrial towns and has a frequent bus service.

A recent inscription carved on the wall of the monument on Stoodley Pike points the direction of the Pennine Way, which now descends east on a clear path (obscure initially), passing the best water-source since leaving Edale, complete with stone trough, to a corner of walls. Over the stile, immediately cross the next wall at a gap and aim for a prominent cairn. Thereafter the route is indefinite for half a mile, but the territory ahead can be surveyed from here and the farm of Lower Rough Head identified. Follow the map closely. At the farm a good road is joined and a pleasant descent made through birch woods, with a charming view across the steep-sided valley to the heights of Heptonstall, crowned by a church. A refreshing change!

HEBDEN BRIDGE 1 (Bus service)

ROAD A 646 TODMORDEN 2¼

canal

R Calder

Callis Wood

Fosters × Stone

Foster's Stone (a jutting crag) is seen high on the left when the road turns due west. The next thing to look for is PIGS. Wandering loose amongst the undergrowth. Be ready to lift your skirts and run.

Edge End (farm)

farm road

Lower Rough Head (farm)

stiles

stile

This old cart-track has the ambitious name of London Road

Dog Stones

Stoodley Pike

spring

stile

A return to trees — and civilisation

*Map very slightly revised 1994, to show new route through Callis Wood.

LANCASHIRE AND YORKSHIRE (W.R.)

The Monument on Stoodley Pike

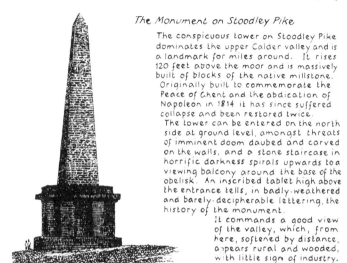

The conspicuous tower on Stoodley Pike dominates the upper Calder valley and is a landmark for miles around. It rises 120 feet above the moor and is massively built of blocks of the native millstone. Originally built to commemorate the Peace of Ghent and the abdication of Napoleon in 1814 it has since suffered collapse and been restored twice.

The tower can be entered on the north side at ground level, amongst threats of imminent doom daubed and carved on the walls, and a stone staircase in horrific darkness spirals upwards to a viewing balcony around the base of the obelisk. An inscribed tablet high above the entrance tells, in badly-weathered and barely-decipherable lettering, the history of the monument.

It commands a good view of the valley, which, from here, softened by distance, appears rural and wooded, with little sign of industry.

Cairn on Coldwell Hill, looking to Stoodley Pike

CHELBURN MOOR TO STOODLEY PIKE

Landranger Sheets 109 and 103

139

Stoodley Pike ▮ monument

across

Coldwell Hill

1300

1200

On Stoodley Pike, look back over the route to the tall masts of Bleakedgate Moor overtopping the horizon — it seems ages ago!

1100

1100

1200

cairned track

boundary stone

To the left, along here, is a splendid view of Todmorden and the valley of the Calder.

Langfield Common

(39)

(38)

boundary stone

1200

old quarry

hut (on wheels, so it might have gone)

cairned track

Warland Drain

This sharp bend in the Warland Drain (a concrete waterway) marks the end of the 'artificial walking,' and brings a return to rougher and undulating moorland tracks. A line of cairns leads across the shoulder of Coldwell Hill and so down to Withens Gate, where a surprising flagged footpath is crossed ('turn left if bound for Mankinholes Youth Hostel.) The main route climbs through the old quarry and then a high level escarpment gives a fine walk to the monument on Stoodley Pike.

MANKINHOLES YOUTH HOSTEL

flagged path

Withens Gate

Stoodley Pike comes into view.

(37)

1200

heather

across

cinder path on embankment

1200

Very easy, dry walking continues on wide, rough waterworks roads to the far end of Warland Reservoir, after which the Warland Drain, bringing in water from distant moors, is followed for a mile on an unnecessarily cairned track alongside in heather and rampant crowberry. Nothing is gained, and much is lost, by a short cut across Langfield Common. The scenery is uninspiring until Coldwell Hill is rounded, but it is interesting to note how the reservoirs are fed from alien watersheds by open drains cut into and contouring the hillsides. The stony rise on the right, with a white Ordnance Survey on its summit, is Little Holder Stones: the Warland Drain encircles this hill.

Warland Reservoir

hut

bench mark on end of wall

waterworks road

Light Hazzles Reservoir

(36)

Lancashire is left and Yorkshire W.R. is re-entered, near the hut by Warland Reservoir.

Down on the left is the valley of the Roch and the Summit Pass between Littleborough and Todmorden — the easiest natural route from south Lancashire to west Yorkshire.

Chelburn Moor

1200

WHITE HOLME RESERVOIR

Dead level, most of the way.

143

LANCASHIRE AND YORKSHIRE (W.R)

The White House

*The Roman Road,
Blackstone Edge*

The Ordnance maps
show 'Roman Road —
course of', but there
has been much recent
contention that the
paving thereon, still
remarkably preserved
in places, is not Roman
in origin, the pattern
of construction being
more akin to the early
packhorse roads and
cart roads in use long
before the industrial
revolution called for
new modes of transport.

*Summit rocks,
Blackstone Edge*

BLACKSTONE EDGE TO CHELBURN MOOR

Miniature bridge, Regulating Drain

141

Light Hazzles Edge

Chelburn Moor

Perched boulder, Light Hazzles Edge.

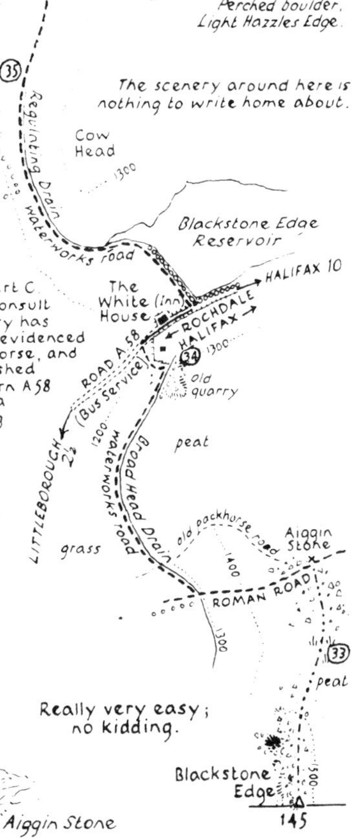

From the Aiggin Stone onwards for three miles the Pennine Way makes its first and only excursion wholly within Lancashire, after which it returns to the West Riding of Yorkshire. This section of three miles, within the domain of Oldham Corporation Waterworks, is the easiest part of the Way, the embankments and catchment drains providing exceptionally good, fast (4 m.p.h.) level walking.

The scenery around here is nothing to write home about.

Cow Head

Blackstone Edge Reservoir

HALIFAX 10

The White House (Inn)

ROCHDALE HALIFAX

old quarry

"The Roof of Lancashire" by Herbert C. Collins (Dent) is a useful book to consult about the Blackstone area. History has been writ large hereabouts and is evidenced by the old roads — Roman, packhorse, and coach — climbing up to the watershed from Littleborough with the modern A 58 and still clearly defined. This is a separate study, but an interesting day could be spent in this vicinity.

peat

The Aiggin Stone, a guide stone marking the summit of the old road, has spent many years in its present tumbled position, and it seems odd that the local archaeologists have not sought to re-erect it. Nearby, some squared blocks were probably mounting steps for horsemen, this being an obvious place for a halt.

grass

old packhorse

Aiggin Stone

ROMAN ROAD

33

peat

Really very easy; no kidding.

Blackstone Edge

Aiggin Stone

145

LANCASHIRE AND YORKSHIRE (W.R)

Ordnance Survey column.
Blackstone Edge

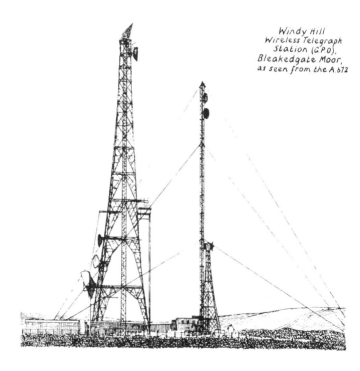

Windy Hill
Wireless Telegraph
Station (GPO),
Bleakedgate Moor,
as seen from the A.672

WHITE HILL TO BLACKSTONE EDGE

Landranger Sheet 109

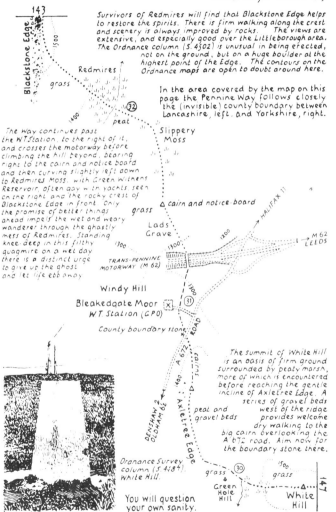

Survivors of Redmires will find that Blackstone Edge helps to restore the spirits. There is firm walking along the crest and scenery is always improved by rocks. The views are extensive, and especially good over the Littleborough area. The Ordnance column (S.4502) is unusual in being erected, not on the ground, but on a huge boulder at the highest point of the Edge. The contours on the Ordnance maps are open to doubt around here.

In the area covered by the map on this page the Pennine Way follows closely the (invisible) county boundary between Lancashire, left, and Yorkshire, right.

143

Blackstone Edge

1500

grass

Redmires

peat

(32)

Slippery Moss

The Way continues past the W.T. Station, to the right of it, and crosses the motorway before climbing the hill beyond, bearing right to the cairn and notice board and then curving slightly left down to Redmires Moss, with Green Withens Reservoir, often gay with yachts seen on the right and the rocky crest of Blackstone Edge in front. Only the promise of better things ahead impels the wet and weary wanderer through the ghastly mess of Redmires. Standing knee-deep in this filthy quagmire on a wet day there is a distinct urge to give up the ghost and let life ebb away.

1400

△ cairn and notice-board

grass

HALIFAX 11 →

Lads' Grave

1300

1200

1300

→ M62 LEEDS

TRANS-PENNINE MOTORWAY (M 62)

1300

Windy Hill

Bleakedgate Moor

W.T. Station (G.P.O.)   ☒   (31)

County boundary stone

1400   A 672 ROAD

△ cairns

DENSHAW 2 OLDHAM 6½

Axletree Edge

The summit of White Hill is an oasis of firm ground surrounded by peaty marsh, more of which is encountered before reaching the gentle incline of Axletree Edge. A series of gravel beds west of the ridge provides welcome dry walking to the big cairn overlooking the A 672 road. Aim now for the boundary stone there.

peat and gravel beds

Ordnance Survey column (S.4784). White Hill.

You will question your own sanity.

grass   (30)   1500

Green Hole Hill   grass

△   White Hill

147

Map revised 1994 to show the crossing over the M62.

LANCASHIRE AND YORKSHIRE (W.R.)

Packhorse Roads across the Pennines

Centuries ago, long before the making of the fine trans-Pennine roads in present use, the considerable trade in merchandise between Lancashire and Yorkshire was conveyed by packhorses and carts travelling on made ways across the moorlands. These, where not converted into modern highways, can still be traced although now deteriorated by disuse into rutted grooves. Typical of many in this area, and marked by occasional stone uprights, is the Marsden Packhorse Road.

Northern Rotcher

Note the perched boulder →

The Dinner Stone

The Ammon Wrigley Memorial Stone

Ammon Wrigley (1861-1946) was a much-revered writer and poet whose love of the country around his native Saddleworth shone in all his works. The rock commemorating his name is the scene of an annual ceremony in his honour.

MILLSTONE EDGE TO WHITE HILL
Landranger Sheets 110 and 109

Sheet 102 has given continuous service
since leaving Edale, but may now, after
crossing the A 640, be stored away until
the walk ends. Its further use will be to
evoke happy and satisfying memories.

slake Linsgreave Head

White Hill

1500

grass

Lancashire-Yorkshire boundary joined.

HUDDERSFIELD 10

1400   stake

The WT masts
on Bleakedgate
are seen directly
ahead from the
top of Rapes Hill.

*The climb
over Rapes Hill is slight,
and a wall gives
direction to the
crossing of a shallow
depression, with a view
downstream of
Readycon Dean Reservoir.*

(29)   o tarn

Rapes Hill

grass

stone
(waterworks)

boundary
1400 stone.

boundary
stone   MARSDEN

1400

ROAD A 640
ROCHDALE
HUDDERSFIELD
(No Bus Service)

DENSHAW 2

Little Moss

grass

Oldgate Nick

1400   Oldgate Moss

From Oldgate Moss and
Little Moss, a view of
the upper Colne Valley
opens up in the east.
The very conspicuous
white building on the
A 640, a mile away, is
Buckstones House, the
scene of an unsolved
double murder in 1903.

*At Northern Rotcher the track turns
north and crosses peat to a small
watercourse. Here leave the track
(which continues on the same contour)
and follow the grassy bank of the
stream slightly uphill to a cairn on
the watershed. Now aim a little
west of north, skirting the
conspicuous scree-slope of
Oldgate Nick and cross
Little Moss to the road,
joining it where an old
pack horse trail goes off
east to Marsden.*

grass and heather

(28)

1400   peat

Northern
Rotcher   peat

1300

The view from the
Ordnance column is
good, the sharp fall
of land to the west
permitting an aerial
view of Castleshaw
and its reservoirs
(Roman Camp near)
and the industrial
valleys beyond.
Southeast are
the rolling moors
crossed from
Black Hill, and
northwest are
those still to
be crossed.

*From the Ordnance column to Northern
Rotcher there is a simple and interesting
promenade with a good view throughout
and the rare pleasure of a dry and stony
track, along the edge of a vast and naked
peat moor. The rock formations are good,
but too small and scattered for serious
climbing, and the escarpment is more
imaginary than real. (Standedge
should not be confused with
Stanage Edge near Sheffield).
Still, this is a nice section.*

cairns

Dinner Stone
Ammon Wrigley memorial
O.S. column S. 1402 △

Easy at first, becoming rougher

YORKSHIRE (W.R)

The top of Millstone Edge

Pule Hill

Although they are unseen
on this walk, at Standedge
we are in the area of some
notable civil engineering
works of the last century.
Directly beneath the road
cutting, but about 600 feet
down, are three tunnels:
the longest canal tunnel
in the country (5415 yards)
and two railway tunnels
each also over 3 miles in
length, all linking Diggle
and Marsden. The road
too is a main artery of
the industrial zones east
and west of the Pennines
and carries a big volume
of heavy traffic across
the moors.

Standedge Cutting, looking east

Footbridge,
Black Moss Reservoir

BLACK MOSS RESERVOIR to MILLSTONE EDGE

Landranger Sheet 110

This section is easy, compared with what has recently been endured. There is a simple rise from the embankment of Black Moss Reservoir to a cairn on Rocher Moss and then a gentle decline, the busy road and Redbrook Reservoir now being in sight ahead. An excellent track, formerly a packhorse road, is joined and this ascends a little to run along the edge of the cutting of the A62, its terminus being somewhat obscured by road works. Across a car park is Peter's Café, which caters for lorry drivers on weekdays, providing quick meals and drinks, and is quite willing to do the same for hungry pedestrians who are able to pay the modest prices and do not criticise the furnishings. At Standedge one is back to civilisation again, and this is true even if Peter's Café is entered. Life may be a bit raw here but the food is well cooked. Like Mario, now only a blissful memory, Peter deserves the P.W. Medal.

The rough unfenced lane opposite the café soon brings a choice of routes, left or right, and, with an eye on the map, it matters little which is taken on this easy ground. Broken walls are crossed to reach Millstone Edge, in rather more exciting surroundings, weathered rocks forming a small escarpment on the left. A stony track leads to the Ordnance column.

**

Map revised 1994.

At Standedge, consider the hour and the condition of the blisters. If the day started at Crowden, most walkers will now have had enough and be ready for a bed. There are roadside inns not far distant and small towns within quick reach, both east and west, with the help of the bus service.

Easy walking; not much up and down.

To the north-west of Black Moss Reservoir, the Pennine Way now descends to join a good path near a stream crossing. This is a much better defined route than the original badly eroded line.

Having crossed the A62, the route follows a sandy track which curves left for 100 yards to meet a junction. One hundred yards beyond, the route turns right, by a small quarry.

The weir, Blakeley Clough

Footbridge, Wessenden Brook

Page amended 1994.

Landranger Sheet 110

Cloudbursts and storms on the peat moors carve deep channels of escape for surplus water in the soft ground. These miniature ravines are locally known as groughs (pronounced gruffs) and normally do not carry streams near their source. Erosion is a continuous process, the steep banks being loose and crumbly and often fantastically sculptured into unstable overhangs. There is no roothold for vegetation and the black earth lies exposed to the elements.

Peat grough.

The Cotton Famine Road (on the original route).

There is a sad reminder on Featherbed Moss of the darkest days of industrial depression in this locality. The long straight ditch or dyke across the moor north of the Greenfield-Holmfirth road received its name from the work its construction gave to people during the Cotton Famine. Although now swampy and overgrown, and unrecognisable as a road, its course is clearly defined and can be followed for several miles. The contrast with the modern road nearby is complete. They belong to different ages.

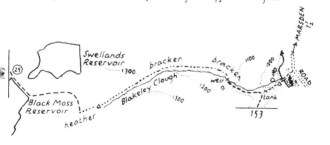

Hard labour, and confusing in mist

After passing a covered water tank, the path follows the south bank of Blakeley Clough, crossing to the north bank at a weir. As the ground levels out, the route turns right, passing between the reservoirs of Black Moss and Swellands.

Map and page revised 1994.

Wessenden

Wessenden is a side-branch of the Colne Valley, a rural backwater of industrial Yorkshire, well known to the people who live in the busy area between Marsden and Huddersfield, for whom it provides a restful and pleasant retreat, but to few others. Once pastoral, this little dale is now occupied by four reservoirs, which have not detracted from its charm.

It is serviced by a road from Marsden, its house has a reputation for good hospitality, its waterfall is a scenic attraction, an open field by the stream is an ideal playground; so that on summer weekends there is activity here and some disturbance of the peaceful scene.

The reservoirs are owned by Huddersfield Corporation, who have imposed few restrictions and whose paths give access to rough moorland But plantings of rhododendrons are a freak decoration, and out of tune with the landscape. The main natural attraction is a lofty and attractive waterfall just opposite to Wessenden Lodge, carrying a feeder down rocky channels overhung by clumps of exotic bloom, where native rowans would look far better. The heavy stonefalls beneath the cascades suggest however that the purpose to be served by the rhododendrons is less to provide a garden than to prevent further erosion on a decaying cliff.

Cotton grass

Cloudberry

Wessenden Lodge, providing refreshments and meals, is a handsome but uncharacteristic house in a pleasant setting and in its own grounds, at the end of the road. It is one of the very few places of refreshment that actually coincides with the official route of the Pennine Way in the southern section.

Page revised 1994.

WESSENDEN HEAD TO WESSENDEN

Landranger Sheet 110

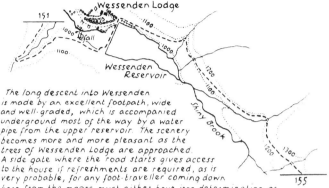

The long descent into Wessenden is made by an excellent footpath, wide and well-graded, which is accompanied underground most of the way by a water pipe from the upper reservoir. The scenery becomes more and more pleasant as the trees of Wessenden Lodge are approached. A side gate where the road starts gives access to the house if refreshments are required, as is very probable, for any foot-traveller coming down here from the moors must either have iron determination or empty pockets to pass by without calling. (The next place offering food is at Standedge, two hours further).

Cross over the dam retaining Wessenden Reservoir and turn right along a level path that follows a contour round a steep-sided valley, crossing it below a waterfall.

Wessenden Lodge

Suspended pool and stony channel on Black Hill

Waterfall
Issue Clough

Having crossed the summit-peat and lived to tell the tale, the deep ravine of Issue Clough is noticed starting to carve its way down on the right. Instead of following the recognised route, parallel to the stream and steeply downhill, descend in a more northerly direction to make sure of 'hitting' the boundary ditch (which is not apparent nearer the stream) and accompany this straight to the A 635, crossing the deeply-cut Dean Clough by a down-and-up scramble and the gentler Reap Hill Clough by a cleverly-contrived track.

EMERGENCY ROUTE FROM BLACK HILL (in case of accident or vile weather or fedupness with the whole idea of doing the Pennine Way): The quickest way off to a road is east, then southeast, to the Holme Moss TV Station, the mast of which is a perfect guide (unless obscured by mist). Beyond, 300 yards further, is the Holmfirth-Woodhead road, A 6024.

Page revised 1994.

BLACK HILL TO WESSENDEN HEAD

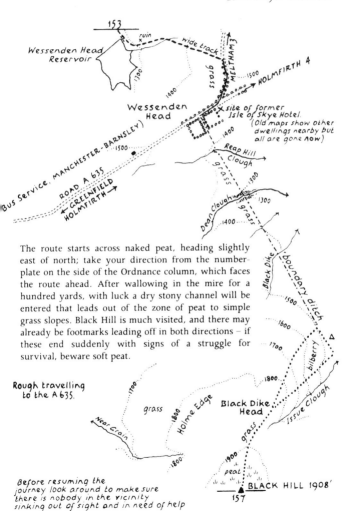

The route starts across naked peat, heading slightly east of north; take your direction from the number-plate on the side of the Ordnance column, which faces the route ahead. After wallowing in the mire for a hundred yards, with luck a dry stony channel will be entered that leads out of the zone of peat to simple grass slopes. Black Hill is much visited, and there may already be footmarks leading off in both directions – if these end suddenly with signs of a struggle for survival, beware soft peat.

Rough travelling to the A635.

Before resuming the journey look around to make sure there is nobody in the vicinity sinking out of sight and in need of help

Map revised 1994.

Black Hill is well named. The broad top really is black. It is not the only fell with a summit of peat, but no other shows such a desolate and hopeless quagmire to the sky. This is peat naked and unashamed. Nature fashioned it, but for once has no suggestion for clothing it. Nothing can grow in this acid waste. There is no root-hold in this sea of ooze. In the flutings and ripplings of the surface of the dunes, caused by the action of rain and wind, a certain strange beauty, a patterned sculpturing beyond the skill of man, must, however, be conceded. But it is a frightening place in bad weather, a dangerous place after heavy rain. It is NOT a place to visit unaccompanied, especially after prolonged rainy weather, because of the risk of becoming trapped or even entombed in the seepage hollows, where the wet peat closes over and grips submerged legs like a vice.

The Ordnance column occupies a tiny island of firm ground in the middle of an undulating sea of black mud, and the surveyors who built it must have been mightily relieved when measurements confirmed that this green oasis was in fact the highest point, for in no other place on the wide summit could a solid footing have been found: it is perhaps unkind to suspect that there are a few slightly higher surfaces nearby.

At 1908', Black Hill is the highest land in Cheshire, the county boundary with Yorkshire crossing the summit. It is overtopped by some hundreds of feet by the TV mast on Holme Moss, a mile away and on wholly Yorkshire ground.

Black Hill from Laddow

LADDOW ROCKS TO BLACK HILL   Landranger Sheet 110

The mound forming the actual summit of Black Hill is named
SOLDIERS LUMP on Ordnance maps, this being derived from
the visits of members of the triangulation party, the Corps
of Royal Engineers. An examination of the mound in 1841
revealed the framework timbers for the
36" Great Ramsden theodolite used in the
original triangulation, which began in 1784.
This magnificent instrument is now on display
at the Science Museum, Kensington. (Information
kindly supplied by the Ordnance Survey).

If travelling north-to-south, i.e from Black Hill to
Crowden, care must be taken on the summit plateau
to steer a course between Meadowgrain Clough
and streams flowing north,
bearing in mind that this
watershed occurs not on the
top of Black Hill but on Dun Hill,
half a mile southwest. This is
difficult to locate in mist.

As the path follows the
left bank of Crowden
Great Brook, the valley
opens out into rolling
moorland and the
walking is tedious
on marshy ground.

Crowden Great Brook,
after being closely
accompanied for a mile,
is joined on the right by
Meadowgrain Clough, and here
left for a beeline northeast over a
weary mile of peaty ground to the top of
Black Hill, which, unfortunately, has no merit
to reward the effort.

155
BLACK HILL
1908'   peat
          1900
          O.S column
          S 2958

20 Dun Hill

Grains
Moss   peaty
        grass
        1700
    1800
Meadowgrain Clough

19

Crowden Great Brook

Castles

Crowden Great Brook

From Laddow Rocks the upper path continues clearly
for a third of a mile without loss of height, thereafter
becoming intermittent and finally indistinct on steeper
ground as it declines towards the lower path.

A wet and weary trudge

159

Map revised 1994.

Laddow Rocks

looking north

the overhang,
north end

Crowden's landscape of fields and trees and scattered cottages is a pleasant relief after the high-level crossing from Edale. It is obviously a place to break the journey overnight, the country beyond being inhospitable and requiring an early morning start. Accommodation is limited to the Crowden Youth Hostel, a newly reconstructed and well-equipped building half a mile off route: this opens its doors to all passing travellers for the provision of refreshments (10 a.m.- 5 p.m.) and reserves beds for non-members.

Crowden is Manchester-in-the-country, the Corporation's reservoirs and ancillary works dominating the scene and, as in so many areas 'acquired' by Big Brother from the individual, there is evidence of neglect and an air of decay in the uncultivated pastures, derelict buildings and crumbling walls. Manchester has, however, done a good service by providing Pennine Way signposts across its land, although one suspects that the motive is not so much to help the walker as to see him off the premises as quickly as possible.

Much of the Crowden valley is used as a rifle range, red flags indicating that the firing squad is operating — a circumstance of which all in the vicinity except the totally deaf are already fully aware.

Crowden Hostel

The Greenfield path is left on the rim of Laddow Rocks, at a cairn, in favour of a clear track along the edge of the cliffs. There are good views here, back over the valley to Bleaklow and Kinder Scout. Black Hill forms a long flat skyline northeast: it is identifiable by the mast of the television station on Holme Moss to its right.

In the original edition, an alternative route was shown passing to the east of Laddow Rocks. However, this is not a public right of way and only the official route should be used as shown on this revised map.

The Ordnance map indicates the route of the Pennine Way out of Crowden as proceeding by Hey Edge and Westend Moss to Black Hill. This section has been amended (as from August 1966) and the approved line now makes use of the good path heading for Greenfield as far as the edge of Laddow Rocks, beyond which it follows Crowden Great Brook upstream and finally aims northeast to Black Hill.

Laddow Rocks is among the best known of the gritstone climbing areas and a place of popular resort. A cave below the overhang at the north end is a perfect refuge in bad weather.

The original route was more direct, safer in mist, and provided a better climb.

The route at the beginning of this page is a new right of way and passes through a pinewood and up some steps before crossing the A628. A track branches left (PW sign) and then, after a wood is passed on your right, the Pennine Way turns sharply to the left. The track continues straight on to Crowden Youth Hostel.

A nice climb on a good path

Map revised 1994.

Torside Clough and Torside Reservoir, from the A 628

Reaps Farm

BLEAKLOW HEAD TO TORSIDE

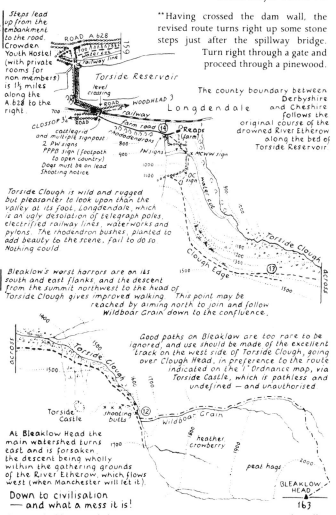

Steps lead
up from the
embankment
to the road.
Crowden
Youth Hostel
(with private
rooms for
non members)
is 1½ miles
along the
A.628 to the
right.

ROAD A 628

Torside Reservoir

level crossing

CLOSSOP 3¾ ROAD

cattlegrid
and multiple signpost:
2 PW signs
PPPD sign (footpath
to open country)
Dogs must be on lead
Shooting notice

Torside Clough is wild and rugged
but pleasanter to look upon than the
valley at its foot, Longdendale, which
is an ugly desolation of telegraph poles,
electrified railway lines, waterworks and
pylons. The rhododendron bushes, planted to
add beauty to the scene, fail to do so.
Nothing could

Bleaklow's worst horrors are on its
south and east flanks, and the descent
from the summit northwest to the head of
Torside Clough gives improved walking.

**Having crossed the dam wall, the
revised route turns right up some stone
steps just after the spillway bridge.
Turn right through a gate and
proceed through a pinewood.

The county boundary between
Derbyshire
and Cheshire
follows the
original course of the
drowned River Etherow
along the bed of
Torside Reservoir

WOODHEAD 3

Longdendale

Reaps (farm)

rhododendrons

PW signs

MCWW sign

OC sign

Water Cut

Torside Clough

Clough Edge

across

This point may be
reached by aiming north to join and follow
Wildboar Grain down to the confluence.

Good paths on Bleaklow are too rare to be
ignored, and use should be made of the excellent
track on the west side of Torside Clough, going
over Clough Head, in preference to the route
indicated on the 1" Ordnance map, via
Torside Castle, which is pathless and
undefined — and unauthorised.

across

Torside Clough

Torside
Castle

shooting
butts

Wildboar Grain

heather
crowberry

peat hags

BLEAKLOW
HEAD
163

At Bleaklow Head the
main watershed turns
east and is forsaken,
the descent being wholly
within the gathering grounds
of the River Etherow, which flows
west (when Manchester will let it).

Down to civilisation
— and what a mess it is!

*From Bleaklow Head the route now goes NNE to a stone waymark. Follow
posts to the north, then north-west, and finally to the west along the north
side of Wildboar Grain.   Map revised 1994.

Wain Stones

The summit of Bleaklow Head

Nature's Sculpture ...." The Kiss"

(This is the only bit of sex in the book)

Bleaklow Head is the western extremity of a 2000' contour extending two miles to Bleaklow Stones in the east — an inhospitable wilderness of peatbogs over which progress on foot is very arduous. The Pennine Way in fact lets walkers off lightly, touching the fringe only of this black desert. Nobody loves Bleaklow. All who get on it are glad to get off.

Devils Dike

Doctor's Gate

SNAKE ROAD to BLEAKLOW HEAD

On the flat and peaty and indefinite wilderness of the Bleaklow plateau there is no awareness of being on a ridge at all, but in fact the principal watershed of northern England bisects its southern slope, although seemingly with considerable indecision. Proof of this is found at the narrow strip of land at the col (in a hollow) where Crooked Clough and Hern Clough are only a few yards apart. Crooked Clough is aiming for the Irish Sea, and Hern Clough for the North Sea. Here is the main watershed, obviously, but although this is clear on a map it is not at all clear on the ground, which hereabouts is a confusing labyrinth of peat bogs and groughs. Navigation is difficult here. It should not be assumed that a stream can be selected on the map and followed: even if identifiable, many streams are often no more than slimy and deep channels in the soft ground, and may be gluey rather than watery. Nor, in this wilderness of peat, should one whoop with joy upon coming across footprints, which too often do not indicate a track but merely the erratic wanderings of some unhappy wretch as hopelessly lost as yourself.

**Substantial improvements have been made to this section of the route and the path is now easy to follow with stone markers. Map revised 1994.

Doctor's Gate, much trodden by 20th century walkers, was originally a Roman road linking the forts of Navio, near Castleton, and Ardotalia, near Glossop.

Roll your pants up above your knees

BLEAKLOW HEAD 2060'

Wain Stones (11)

161

peat bogs

2000

Dowstone Clough × post

Hern Stones

1900

peat bogs

Hern Clough

Lives have been lost on Bleaklow

1800

col (10)

peat bogs

1800

1800

peat

peat

Alport Low × two posts

1800

← path enters dike

Devil's Dike, a good direction-pointer, is a remarkably straight channel. The usual path is on the east bank but the floor of the dike also has a track, which may be preferred. *

Crooked Clough

1700

Devils Dike

peat bilberry

1700

← path enters dyke

DOCTOR'S GATE (ROMAN ROAD) GLOSSOP 4 ←

peaty grass

SNAKE INN 2½

peaty grass

GLOSSOP 4 ←

PW sign × SNAKE ROAD A 57

SNAKE INN 2¼

165

This section is commonly considered the toughest part of the Pennine Way. It is certainly mucky, too often belaboured by rain and wind, and wierd and frightening in mist. But cheer up. There is worse to follow.

Nature in the raw

*The route now officially passes along the floor of the dike, and the surface has been much improved. At the end of the dike, the path follows the stream up Hern Clough and then continues to just east of the Wain Stones. On this revised route, the Hern Stones are away on the left.

above:
A peat grough on
Featherbed Moss

left:
Gritstone boulders
on the western edge
of Kinder Scout

The western buttresses
of Kinder Scout

KINDER SCOUT TO SNAKE ROAD

Landranger Sheet 110

The long drag from Mill Hill to the Snake Road is featureless and tedious, and although the walking is fairly level and technically easy, the ground is sloppy. There is a good view of the northern edges of Kinder all the way. Beyond Glead Hill the top of the Snake Road, which is usually identifiable by parked cars, is in sight continuously with Bleaklow to its left.

163

PW sign

OC sign ×

SNAKE ROAD A 57

→ SNAKE INN 2¼

Infrequent bus service summer only (MANCHESTER - SHEFFIELD)

GLOSSOP

1600

peat channels

Featherbed Moss

peat channels

crowberry

1700

Featherbed Moss is a maze of narrow peat channels, some of them mere slits cloaked by vegetation. It is a potential leg-breaker. Go slowly and take care.

across

1700

⑧

across

1700

peaty grass bilberry crowberry

line of posts

Moss Castle

peat

post

× post

⑦ Glead Hill

1700

'aeroplane bridge'

peaty grass

1700

The journey from Mill Hill to Moss Castle (much moss, no castle) is deadly dull. A fragment of aeroplane fusillage brought into use to bridge a bog is the only item of interest.

The enjoyable walk along the escarpment northwest from Kinder Downfall comes to an end where cairns indicate the place to descend, rather steeply, to the broad path, almost a highway, crossing the depression below en route between Hayfield and the Snake Inn. Cross this and ascend a gentle incline to the post on Mill Hill (no mill, not much hill). Here it is important to note the right-angled turn northeast with the top of the Snake Road as the next objective.

grass

ASHOP CLOUGH AND SNAKE INN

Mill Hill 1761'

⑥

× post

signpost

1700

peaty grass

1700

1900

1900

grass

WILLIAM CLOUGH AND HAYFIELD

The Hayfield-Snake Inn path at its summit (where crossed by the Pennine Way)

The attractions of the Kinder escarpments are unique. Along the edges the walking is dry and firm, with little rise or fall, over terrain marked by weathered boulders and surfaced by sand and gravel, a natural terrace between the naked peat of the plateau and the gritstone cliffs. One's appetite is whetted for more, and in fact there is a recognised circuit of the Kinder Edges well worth walking. But not this trip. No time! Someday in the future

boulders and gravel

KINDER SCOUT

⑤

1900

1800

2000

1600

167

A profound deterioration in quality.

*Map revised 1994. The new paved route bypasses, on higher ground, some of the worst groughs of Featherbed Moss.

Kinder Downfall

This drawing looks an untidy mess
but so does Kinder Downfall

The head of Kinder Downfall

Kinder Gates

Edale Rocks

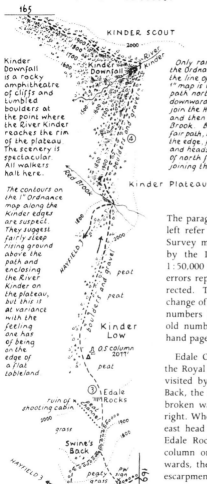

KINDER SCOUT

2000

River Kinder

1900 1800 1700

Kinder Downfall

1600

Kinder Downfall is a rocky amphitheatre of cliffs and tumbled boulders at the point where the River Kinder reaches the rim of the plateau. The scenery is spectacular. All walkers halt here.

Only rarely can the impeccable accuracy of the Ordnance maps be questioned, but surely the line of the footpath over Kinder Low on the 1" map is wrongly plotted? This indicates the path north of the trig point 2077 as inclining downwards, losing some 300 feet in height, to join the Hayfield path coming up on the left, and then a big curve eastwards to cross Red Brook. But in fact north of the trig point a fair path, becoming very clear, contours along the edge, following the natural lie of the land, and heads directly on a course slightly east of north for the crossing of Red Brook, there joining the Hayfield path with little descent.

The contours on the 1" Ordnance map along the Kinder edges are suspect. They suggest fairly steep rising ground above the path and enclosing the River Kinder on the plateau, but this is at variance with the feeling one has of being on the edge of a flat tableland.

1800

Red Brook

Kinder Plateau

HAYFIELD ➔

2000

boulders and gravel

peat

peat

Kinder Low

△ OS column 2077'

peat

③ Edale Rocks

ruin of shooting cabin

2000

grass

1900

1800

Swine's Back

HAYFIELD ➔

peaty grass

PW sign

Edale Cross

×10

169

The paragraph above and the one bottom left refer to the inch-to-a-mile Ordnance Survey map which has been superseded by the Landranger map at a scale of 1 : 50,000 or 1¼ inches to a mile. Both the errors reported here have now been corrected. The change of scale meant a change of sheet layout, and the new sheet numbers have been substituted for the old numbers at the top of all the right-hand pages in this book.

Edale Cross is a boundary marker for the Royal Forest of the Peak and may be visited by a short diversion. At Swine's Back, the route passes through a gap in a broken wall and follows the wall to the right. When the wall curves round to the east head north, passing to the right of Edale Rocks and to the left of the OS column on Kinder Low. From here onwards, the route follows the crest of the escarpment to Kinder Downfall.

The first highlight of the journey

Kinder Gates, illustrated on the opposite page, is situated on the River Kinder half a mile above the Downfall. It is no longer on the route of the Pennine Way.

Page revised 1994.

Ruins of
Edale Head House

Big cairn
near the top of the Hayfield path

Footbridge (formerly
a packhorse bridge)
at the bottom of
Jacob's Ladder

Not until reaching the footbridge at the bottom of Jacob's Ladder, 2½ miles after leaving Edale, does the route forsake the valleys for the hills.

From Upper Booth, a charming hamlet embowered in fine trees and having some unusual features (note the postbox in the farmyard), a tarred road goes upvalley to Lee House and there, through two gates, gives place to a wide and distinct path. On the bend before the footbridge, the view ahead, although severely confined, shows several striking tors on the skyline: weathered gritstone rocks, more of which will be seen, and more intimately, later in the walk.

Jacob's Ladder presents no difficulties and the 'dangerous ground' warning signs seem oddly incongruous to anyone with experience of Rossett Gill or Lord's Rake or Mickledore in the Lake District; in fact, the exit from Grindsbrook Clough on the main route is rougher.

Above Jacob's Ladder a wide path heads west alongside a broken wall, this being an old but still much trodden bridle road to Hayfield

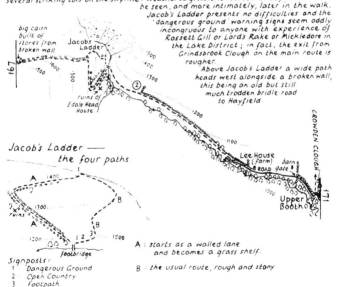

big cairn built of stones from broken wall

Jacobs Ladder

ruins of Edale Head House

Jacob's Ladder —
the four paths

Lee House (Farm)
barn
ROAD gate

Upper Booth

CROWDEN CLOUGH

A : starts as a walled lane and becomes a grass shelf.

B : the usual route, rough and stony

Signposts:
1 Dangerous Ground
2 Open Country
3 Footpath

Keep moving. Too early yet for a rest.

Page revised 1994.

Waterfall,
Grinds Brook

The Pennine Way starts at Grindsbrook Booth, the village of the parish of Edale, a tiny cluster of neat cottages, with an inn and a shop, beautifully situated in rural surroundings at the foot of Kinder Scout.

Edale has no bus service, but several trains stop daily at the station (Manchester-Sheffield line). Overnight accommodation is limited. There is a camp site, and a Youth Hostel two miles east at Rowland Cote.

The Peak District National Park guide, obtainable at the Information Centre, gives a splendid introduction to the area, which attracts crowds of visitors at weekends. If you can, arrive midweek.

The Start

Well now, you will have arrived in Edale scarcely able to believe that the Great Adventure is about to start at last.

After months of planning, of studying maps and reading books, of counting your money, the day has come. You are in Edale with your boots on, ready to start. You have said your farewells; now you are on your own. You are on your own even though you have companions, for if you arrive in due course at the end of the journey only your own efforts will have got you there. Make no mistake: you are going to suffer, you are going to get wet through, you are going to feel miserable and wish you had never heard of the Pennine Way. But there will be days of bright sunshine too, and moments of fun; many interesting experiences and a vision of beauty in desolate places will be your reward.

If you start, don't give up, or you will be giving up at difficulties all your life.

Entrance to footbridge
Grinds Brook

Right then, let's get going. You have checked your rucksack and made sure you haven't forgotten anything vital. Kirk Yetholm, we are on our way. Be seeing you soon.

The Pennine Way starts at the cluster of buildings named Grindsbrook Booth centred around the Old Nag's Inn. Take a path signed for Upper Booth, Hayfield and the Pennine Way. This runs to the left of the track on the opposite side of the road from the inn. Follow a clear path along the sunken lane and turn left over the second stile, from where the path, now flagged, runs across the fields with Broadleebank Tor on the right.

Continue on the path to a signpost on a grassy rise, go straight on downhill in a south-westerly direction to join a muddy track which leads through Upper Booth Farm. Having passed some old stone troughs, turn right along a metalled lane which crosses Crowden Brook.

The first major objective is Kinder Downfall, on the western edge of Kinder Scout. When this book first appeared there were two approved ways of reaching it. The main route led up Grindsbrook Clough and then crossed a trackless plateau of peat with no guiding landmarks: a bad place in mist and rain. The alternative route, more circuitous and 1½ miles longer, approached the Downfall from the south with the initial help of a good path, but this too had a trackless section although on easier ground. Now only one route is available, as shown below. Before a step is taken, however, a decision has to be made with an eye on the weather. The wisdom of leaving Edale on a wet morning should be debated earnestly. Better a postponement than a postmortem.

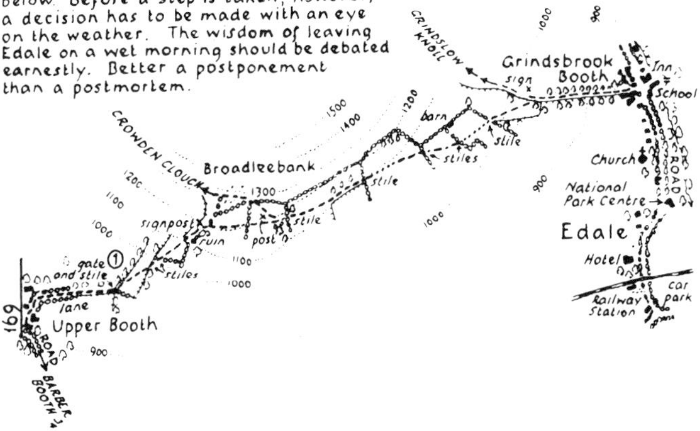

Come out of that tuckshop!.......... Ready now? Let's go!

Page revised 1994.
The two drawings on the facing page depict features which are on the original route up Grindsbrook Clough from which the Pennine Way has now been diverted.

INDEX TO PLACE-NAMES ON THE MAPS

INDEX *continued*

INDEX *continued*

The foregoing index lists only the place-names shown on the maps. Other references to these names, where they occur in the illustrations and notes accompanying the maps, will be found on the same page or the page opposite.

Author's personal notes in conclusion

Well, I'm glad it's finished, I must say. I mean the walking, not the making of the book, which has been very enjoyable. No, I mean the walking, the floundering in glutinous peatbogs, the stumbling in soggy heathers, the squelching in muddy fields. Surely I must have been unlucky about the rain! I spent eighteen months on the Pennine Way, walking it in bits and pieces. Mostly it rained — pouring rain, driving rain, rain that came down like stair-rods. I came to pray not for fine days, which seemed too much to ask, but for gentle and not-too-wetting rain.

My maps became sodden. So did I. On one outing (the crowning ignominy for a seasoned fellwalker) I sought refuge under a lady's umbrella. The rain was awful. There were a few fine days, mere pinpricks in the general gloom, but even then the ground still squirted at every step and paths remained ribbons of water.... I suppose the Pennine Way never dries out. It never did for me.

If I had not had this book to write I doubt whether I would ever have left Lakeland to go wallowing in the mud of the Pennines. My first foray was to Edale and was an abysmal non-success. Four days of non-stop rain. I fled the place. Then I went up to Kirk Yetholm to see what it was like up there. Raining, it was. Solidly, for three days. I fled. To hell with the Pennine Way, I thought — nobody will want to read a book about it, anyway. But I couldn't rid myself of the itch to write it, and gradually later I got moving in between the downpours.

In a macabre sort of way I enjoyed it. Rain is invigorating (somebody once said) and there was a satisfaction in ticking off the miles and in closing the untrodden gaps. I followed no sequence, getting parts done as and when I was given an opportunity of transport. I switched about between the Peak and the Border in a most erratic fashion, collecting miles jealously as a schoolboy collects train numbers. The Pennine Way became a mammoth jigsaw into which I fitted pieces as and when I could. The last piece went into place, completing the picture, only one week before the tragic foot-and-mouth disease closed the countryside and the fells for the winter. I was spared the final straw.

I met a man in my travels who had walked the Pennine Way and suffered only two hours rain: he thought it was great. It can never be great: the final sense of achievement is, as you stagger over the finishing line, but the bliss you feel is the bliss you feel when you stop banging your head against a wall — the day-to-day performance is tedious. It is very interesting as a study of the geography of northern England, but the perambulation itself is dull. Except for the conditions underfoot, the walking is easy and unexciting: there is much up and down work, but contours are gentle. Only the ascent of Penyghent — a brief moment of glory — ranks as top-class fellwalking.

But yes, it is interesting: the variety and gradual changes of scenery make it so. Black moors alternate with green valleys. There are desolate hilltops but pleasant rivers too. The barren uplands give place to woodlands and forests, the moss and bog and heather of the heights to flowery meadows. One walks at first, starting from Edale, on a lofty causeway of gritstone between industrial towns, and it is an odd experience here, crossing the rough desolate moors, to meet the many trans-Pennine roads, busy with traffic: strips of tarmac, pulsating with noise and movement, thrown across the lifeless deserts of peat. Then follows a region of rolling foothills, still bare but less wild, to the pastoral peace of Airedale. There is a too-brief encounter with the fascinating limestone country of Craven, and moors again to the lovely reaches of upper Teesdale. Cross Fell, the summit of the Pennine Way, next dominates the route before being succeeded by further valley-walking. The Roman Wall is reached and inspires the imagination for a few miles before the spruce forests of the Border are entered. A long high traverse of the Cheviot Hills completes the journey. On the way, one sees ancient castles and earthworks, many evidences

of former mining activity, now derelict,
and places with literary or historical
associations.   Interesting too are the
changes in local dialects as you pass
from one district to another, the way
the brooks become becks and then burns,
the different breeds of sheep from Peak
to Border...... Yes, it is all interesting,
but weeping skies deaden enthusiasm,
and fine weather is needed for a full
appreciation of the Pennine Way. In
any conditions, however, it will always
be an invigorating exercise for the limbs,
a complete change of environment, the
perfect tonic for a jaded mind and a
cure for urban depression. If you want
to "get away from it all", here, ideally,
is the escape. You can't get further from
the familiar than on the Pennine Way.
You live for a time in a new world,
and you forget the other.

My choice of the highlights of the walk,
taking them as they come, is as follows:

Kinder Downfall
Gordale Scar (off·route)
Malham Cove
Hull Pot, Penyghent (off·route)
Ling Gill
Hardrow Force (off·route)
High Force
Cauldron Snout
High Cup
The Roman Wall
Hareshaw Linn (off·route)

Those are the spectacular highlights, of general appeal, but every walker of the Pennine Way will have his own special favourite memory. Mine is the sight of a limestone pinnacle on Penyghent, seen in April sunshine, draped with purple saxifrage. But the greatest emotional highlight, for most walkers, will be the first glimpse of Kirk Yetholm as the hill is topped from the Halterburn valley.

I want to give support to a cause that Harry Appleyard, like a prophet in the wilderness, has been pleading for years. Along the Pennine Way, even in the most unlikely places, one notes with concern the grabbing of open land by a growing number of Government Departments and nationalised undertakings and other bureaucratic bodies. Quite vast areas are sealed off, and access is barred, on the pretext that the land is waste and of little value anyway. Sheep and walkers, who formerly had freedom to roam, are being confined and channelled within permitted areas, and being prohibited, under threats and penalties, from doing (a) this, (b) that and (c) the other.

CLEAR OFF
YOU CAN'T
COME IN HERE!
ITS OURS.

Ancient privileges are being filched. On the Pennines wide tracts of country are commandeered by the Air Ministry and the War Ministry; once-open uplands have become impenetrable forests; lush valleys are being swallowed by reservoirs; even the nature reserves are loud in their prohibitions. Yorkshire folk used to build stone towers on their hilltops, but now all kinds of fancy contraptions in wire enclosures desecrate the skylines. The Pennine Way, in fact, does jolly well to steer a free route through all the prison fences. The former much-abused private landowners, who at least knew and loved their countryside, were saints compared with the present autocrats who dictate their threats from city offices. The latest area to be sacrificed in the name of progress is near Cow Green in upper Teesdale, where a new reservoir is to drown a district of unique botanical interest despite an eruption of protest. You can't win against Big Brother.... The old landowners did at least wear tweeds and heavy boots, and listened to reason, but you can't argue against these gents in pin stripes and patent shoes. It is a democratic country we live in, friends. This is democracy at work. Sometimes it's hard to believe.

Not all walkers are saints, either. You must expect some of the signposts indicated on the maps to be missing when you get there, wantonly destroyed or used for campfires. You must expect opposition, and rightly so, from farmers over whose land you stray — they have work enough to do without repairing walls and fences broken by trespassers. Some of the farmers do not seem to have been consulted sufficiently about the route — it is odd to be asked "where the devil is the Pennine Way?" by the man over whose land it passes.

Talking about farms, the one aspect of the walk I was most apprehensive about, studying maps in advance, was the passage through the innumerable farms on the route. I have never liked farmyards: so much hidden menace lurks there in the form of geese and loose pigs and dogs,

and it is not a bit of use trying to get through unnoticed, on tiptoe — bedlam is loosed at the first squeak of the gate. But I fared well. I was hissed at and barked at but never bitten or butted.

"Please can you tell me where the Pennine Way is?"

I must eat some of my earlier words about solitary walking. I got into trouble for defending, in 'Fellwanderer', solitary walking in the Lake District — which I do not retract — but on the wilder parts of the Pennines it is very desirable to have a companion. On the summit of Black Hill I got absolutely stuck in a peat bog and incapable of doing anything about it, but my escort and a National Park warden, who by the merest chance happened to be within call, managed to drag me out. On Bleaklow, on a day of driving rain and bitter wind, I began to lose all feeling in my legs and had to beat a retreat. On Cam Fell, a freezing east wind near to gale force, so shrivelled some of the body organs necessary for a full and enjoyable life that I feared they were perished forever, but happily their use returned in full flower after a brief rest. Clearly I am not as young as I used to be. Most of the Pennine Way I walked alone, but on the occasions mentioned I was glad to have a companion. You need someone with you in the Pennine wildernesses. I was thrice blessed in my choice of companions: they walked well, they were considerate, and they were nice to have at my side.

One other thing I have forgotten to mention: the grouse moors of the Peak are closed on certain days in the shooting season and may affect the route; see the notices displayed. Foot and mouth epidemics, too, have closed sections of the Pennine Way both in 1966 and 1967.

This book has been completed in a hurry after several delays (due to continuous rain, of course). In the final revision I found three spelling errors, and there are two omissions in the index. I just couldn't be bothered to make the necessary amendments — when a book is written by hand an alteration may involve a re-drafting of the whole page, a matter of four or five hours work; and time was pressing. So I've let them stay in as deliberate mistakes — something to pass the time finding when you are holed up in a cave out of the rain.

Well, I hope you enjoy it, I really do. In a way, I feel a bit sorry for you — but you are almost certain to have an interesting journey in better conditions than I had. The walk will do you good.

You won't come across me anywhere along the Pennine Way.

I've had enough of it.

New Year 1968   A.W.

Limestone pinnacle,
   Penyghent

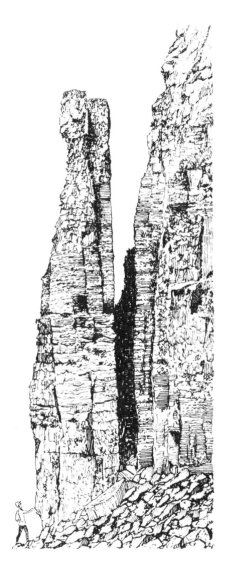

EXCELSIOR !

PART ONE:
Departure from Edale

Reader's LOG OF THE JOURNEY

The remaining pages in this book are provided for the use of readers engaged on the walk.

The route in the Log is divided into sections, mainly for the benefit of those who cannot, or prefer not to, undertake the whole journey at one time. The sections are short, most being suitable for half-day walks, and they are, of course, quite arbitrary and may be shortened or lengthened at will to take account of weather conditions and time available.

Each section, as printed, ends at a motor road, to enable arrangements to be made for transport, if desired.

A walker doing the whole journey at once can ignore these sections: normally, in a full day's travel, he will cover two or more sections and often wish to break his walk for overnight stay at an intermediate point.

The following symbols are used in the Log

✓ : point accessible by car

✗ : road with bus service

N.G.R. : National Grid Reference

Miles { S : in section
        E : from Edale

Times { A : of arrival
        D : of departure

Try to keep your entries neat, please, or the whole book will look untidy. One other thing: you'll be mad if you lose the book when it contains your own personal record of the walk, so enter your name and address in the panel below:

Finder, please return to

*It is advisable to check bus services in advance since there have been many changes since the book was written.

LOG OF THE JOURNEY

Date	Section	NGR	Miles S	Miles E	Times A	Times D	Weather
	✓ Grindsbrook Booth, Edale	SK 123859	1	1			
	Kinder Downfall	SK 082889	4	4			
	Mill Hill	SK 061904	6	6			
	X Road A.57 (Snake Road)	SK 087929	8½	8½			
	Bleaklow Head	SK 092959	2½	11			
	✓ Road B.6105 (Torside)	SK 056980	5¾	14¼			
	X Road A.628	SK 055986	6¼	14¾			
	Laddow Rocks	SE 056014	2¾	17½			
	Black Hill	SE 077047	6	20¾			
	X Road A.635	SE 051063	8¼	23			
	Black Moss Reservoir	SE 033086	2	25			
	X Road A.62 (Standedge)	SE 018095	3	26			
	Millstone Edge	SE 012104	4	27			
	✓ Road A.640	SE 002123	5¾	28¾			
	White Hill	SD 991132	6¾	29¾			
	X Road A.672 (W.T.Station)	SD 983142	7¾	30¾			

Blackstone Edge	SD 973164	2	$32\frac{3}{4}$
X Road A.58 (White House)	SD 969179	$3\frac{1}{4}$	34
Path to Mankinholes Y.H.	SD 968231	$4\frac{1}{2}$	$38\frac{1}{2}$
Stoodley Pike	SD 973242	$5\frac{1}{2}$	$39\frac{1}{2}$
X Road A.646 (Calder Valley)	SD 972265	8	42
X Colden	SD 967287	$1\frac{3}{4}$	$43\frac{3}{4}$
✓ Widdop Road	SD 949320	5	47
Withins	SD 983356	4	51
✓ Colne-Haworth Road	SD 987375	$6\frac{1}{2}$	$53\frac{1}{2}$
✓ Colne-Oakworth Road	SD 988380	$\frac{1}{2}$	54
Ickornshaw Moor	SD 973395	2	$55\frac{1}{2}$
X Road A.6068 (Ickornshaw)	SD 966428	$4\frac{3}{4}$	$58\frac{1}{4}$
X Lothersdale	SD 959459	$2\frac{1}{2}$	$60\frac{3}{4}$
Pinhaw Beacon	SD 944472	$4\frac{1}{4}$	$62\frac{1}{2}$
X Road A.56 (Thornton in Craven)	SD 908486	7	$65\frac{1}{4}$
X Road A.65 (Gargrave)	SD 932541	$4\frac{3}{4}$	70
✓ Airton Bridge	SD 904592	4	74
✓ Hanlith Bridge	SD 900612	$5\frac{1}{4}$	$75\frac{1}{4}$
X Malham	SD 901629	$6\frac{3}{4}$	$76\frac{3}{4}$

LOG OF THE JOURNEY continued

Date	Section	N.G.R.	Miles S	Miles E	Times A	Times D	Weather
	Malham Tarn House	SD 894673	$3\frac{3}{4}$	$80\frac{1}{2}$			
	✓ Arncliffe Road	SD 884692	$5\frac{1}{2}$	$82\frac{1}{4}$			
	Fountains Fell	SD 868719	$2\frac{3}{4}$	85			
	✓ Stainforth-Halton Gill Road	SD 843715	$4\frac{3}{4}$	87			
	Penyghent	SD 839734	$1\frac{1}{2}$	$88\frac{1}{2}$			
	✗ Road B 6479 (Horton in Ribblesdale)	SD 809724	$4\frac{3}{4}$	$91\frac{3}{4}$			
	Sell Gill Holes	SD 812744	$1\frac{1}{2}$	$93\frac{1}{4}$			
	✓ Old Ing Farm	SD 805773	4	$95\frac{3}{4}$			
	Cam End	SD 802805	$6\frac{1}{2}$	$98\frac{1}{4}$			
	✓ Kidhow Gate	SD 830834	$9\frac{1}{4}$	101			
	✗ Road A 684 (Hawes)	SD 873898	$5\frac{3}{4}$	$106\frac{3}{4}$			
	✓ Hardrow	SD 867912	7	108			
	Great Shunner Fell	SD 849973	$5\frac{1}{4}$	$113\frac{1}{4}$			
	✗ Road B 6270 (Thwaite)	SD 892982	9	117			
	✗ Keld	NY 893012	3	120			
	✓ Tan Hill Inn	NY 897067	7	124			

	✓ Sleightholme	NY 955101	4¾	128¾			
	✗ Road A.66 (Pasture End)	NY 956129	6¾	130¾			
	Race Yate	NY 942161	2½	133¼			
	✓ Blackton Bridge	NY 933183	4¼	135			
	✓ Grassholme Bridge	NY 930216	6¾	137½			
	✓ Road B.6276 (Wythes Hill)	NY 924225	7½	138¼			
	✗ Middleton in Teesdale	NY 947254	10¼	141			
	✗ Wynch Bridge	NY 904279	3½	144½			
	High Force	NY 881284	5	146			
	✓ Saur Hill (for Langdon Beck)	NY 854302	8	149			
	Widdybank Farm	NY 837298	1½	150½			
	✓ Cauldron Snout	NY 814287	3¾	152¾			
	✓ Birkdale	NY 804279	1¼	154			
	High Cup	NY 746262	5½	158¼			
	✗ Dufton	NY 690250	9½	162¼			
	Knock Fell	NY 721303	4¾	167			
	✓ Great Dun Fell (end of public road)	NY 717317	5¾	168			
	Cross Fell	NY 687343	2¾	170¾			
	✓ Garrigill	NY 745415	10¾	178¾			

LOG OF THE JOURNEY continued

Date	Section	N.G.R.	Miles S	Miles E	Times A	Times D	Weather
	Sillyhall	NY 721433	2¼	181			
	✗ Road A.686 (Alston)	NY 717462	4	182¾			
	Gilderdale Burn	NY 698479	2¼	185			
	✓ Kirkhaugh	NY 694499	3½	186¼			
	✗ Slaggyford	NY 678525	6	188¾			
	✗ Burnstones	NY 675544	1¾	190½			
	✗ Glendue Bridge	NY 671564	3¼	192			
	✗ Road B.6292 (Lambley)	NY 663586	4¾	193½			
	✓ Kellah Burn	NY 654612	7	195¾			
	Wain Rigg	NY 644628	1¼	197			
	✓ Road A.69 (nr. Greenhead)	NY 651652	3½	199¼			
	✗ Road B.6318 (Thirlwall)	NY 657659	4¼	200			
	Thirlwall Castle	NY 659662	¼	200¼			
	Aesica Roman Fort	NY 703668	4	204			
	Winshields Crag	NY 742676	6¾	206¾			
	✓ Peel Road (for Once Brewed YH)	NY 751676	7¼	207¼			

Hotbank Crags	NY 775685	$2\frac{1}{2}$	$209\frac{3}{4}$
Rapishaw Gap	NY 781686	3	$210\frac{1}{4}$
Housesteads (detour)	NY 790688	$3\frac{3}{4}$	211
Rapishaw Gap	NY 781686	$4\frac{1}{2}$	$211\frac{3}{4}$
✓ Road near Ladyhill	NY 798752	$9\frac{3}{4}$	217
Warks Burn	NY 813772	2	219
✓ Shillington Hall	NY 829801	$4\frac{3}{4}$	$221\frac{3}{4}$
✗ Bellingham	NY 839833	8	225
✓ Road B 6320 (Hareshaw)	NY 842883	4	229
Lough Shaw	NY 844893	$4\frac{3}{4}$	$229\frac{3}{4}$
Deer Play	NY 842903	$5\frac{1}{4}$	$230\frac{1}{4}$
Lord's Shaw	NY 829913	$6\frac{1}{4}$	$231\frac{1}{4}$
✓ Gib Shiel Road	NY 824917	7	232
Padon Hill	NY 817928	$3\frac{3}{4}$	**$232\frac{3}{4}$**
Brownrigg Head	NY 817944	2	234
✓ Rookengate	NY 798956	$3\frac{1}{2}$	$235\frac{1}{2}$
✓ Blakehopeburnhaugh	NT 784001	7	239
✓ Cottonshopeburn Foot	NT 778013	1	240
✗ Byrness, Road A.68	NT 771024	$2\frac{1}{4}$	$241\frac{1}{4}$

LOG OF THE JOURNEY continued

Date	Section	N.G.R	Miles S	Miles E	Times A	Times D	Weather
	Ravens Knowe	NT 781062	2¾	244			
	✓ Chew Green Roman Camps	NT 787086	5¼	246½			
	Lamb Hill	NT 810133	4	250½			
	Beefstand Hill	NT 821143	5	251½			
	Russell's Cairn, Windy Gyle	NT 856153	7¾	254¼			
	* Border Gate, Clennel Street	NT 871161					
	* *vehicular access: Land Rovers only. motor road at Cocklawfoot (2 miles)*		8¾	255¼			
	Cairn Hill west top	NT 897194	3½	258¾			
	The Cheviot *(detour)*	NT 909205	4¾	260			
	Cairn Hill west top	NT 897194	6	261¼			
	The Schil	NT 869223	9	264¼			
	✓ Burnhead	NT 844258	12¼	267½			
	X Kirk Yetholm	NT 827282	2½	270			

RECORD OF ACCOMMODATION USED ON THE WALK

Provision is made below for 20 beds and breakfasts, which assumes that an average of 12 to 15 miles per day will be walked, just about right for a comfortable journey.

Date of arrival	Address	Charge

THE BROTHERHOOD OF THE PENNINE WAY

There is no Pennine Way Club, nor any association with exclusive membership for those who have fully completed the journey and therefore no opportunity to exchange notes except by private arrangement.

During the journey other walkers will be met who are similarly engaged. Acquaintance starts on a common ground and with a mutual interest, for all who meet on the Pennine Way share the same ambition and are impelled by the same challenge.

They are, however, ships that pass in the night.

They will probably never meet again.

Unless, of course, a friendship is born and there is an agreed desire to correspond and swap notes after the journey's end. In such cases this page and the next can be used to record names and addresses. Nicer still if the other fellow would autograph it for you and so provide a more intimate memory of the meeting!

Date of meeting	Name and address	Place of meeting

Date of meeting	Name and address	Place of meeting

EXCELSIOR !

PART TWO:
Arrival at Kirk Yetholm

THAT
BLOODY
WAINWRIGHT!